Praise for
AFTERNOONS WITH MR. HOGAN

"Contains enlightening personal anecdotes and astounding golf tips that will thrill any enthusiast.... Vasquez's unique position and twenty-year relationship with the champion allowed him access to all of Ben Hogan. In an easygoing, conversational writing style, the stories Vasquez related here are the rich fruits of that relationship and should not be missed."
            —*Publishers Weekly*

"A fan's memoir recommended for all golf collections."
            —*Library Journal*

"Much more interesting than anything written by people who didn't know Ben. Excuse me, 'Mr. Hogan.' "
            —Dan Jenkins, friend of Ben Hogan and author of
            Dead Solid Perfect

"As a longtime Hogan PGA staff member, I welcome Jody's book. Most know Mr. Hogan's life story, but few were allowed to see the side of the man I was able to experience. It's a fantastic look into Hogan, the man."
            —Hal Sutton, 2004 USA Ryder Cup captain

"Like Bobby Jones and Old Tom Morris, Ben Hogan added something fundamental—and magical—to the world of golf. His devotion to practice, which for him was an art, and his magnetic, legendary presence at play are part of his legacy. This book adds to what we know about him and, for that reason, may become a golf classic."
            —Michael Murphy, author of *Golf in the Kingdom*
            and *The Kingdom of Shivas Irons*

"Ben Hogan was the most private public figure I have ever known. It's terrific that Jody shares these stories. It would be a shame to look back and only see Hogan's amazing record, yet know nothing of the man, his thoughts, or his beliefs. "

—Lee Trevino, six-time major-championship winner

"Having represented the Ben Hogan Golf Company for over a decade I had a limited opportunity to get to know Mr. Hogan. But I had so many questions that I never had the opportunity to get answered. Jody's insight answers a number of these and sheds light on the complex personality of Mr. Hogan that few ever got to see. This is great reading for all golfers who are curious about the Hogan mystique."

—Tom Kite, fifteen-time Ryder Cup winner and author of *A Fairway to Heaven*

Jody Vasquez shagged balls for Ben Hogan for four years at Shady Oaks Country Club in the 1960s. Vasquez is now a member of the Colonial Country Club, where he serves on the board of governors and the tournament committee for the annual PGA Colonial event, the longest-running site on the PGA Tour and the tournament Hogan won five times. He lives in Fort Worth, Texas.

AFTERNOONS WITH
MR. HOGAN

*A Boy, a Golf Legend,
and the Lessons of a Lifetime*

JODY VASQUEZ

**GOTHAM
BOOKS**

GOTHAM BOOKS
Published by Penguin Group (USA) Inc.
375 Hudson Street, New York, New York 10014, U.S.A.
Penguin Group (Canada), 10 Alcorn Avenue, Toronto, Ontario, Canada M4V 3B2
(a division of Pearson Penguin Canada Inc.); Penguin Books Ltd, 80 Strand, London
WC2R 0RL, England; Penguin Ireland, 25 St Stephen's Green, Dublin 2, Ireland
(a division of Penguin Books Ltd); Penguin Group (Australia), 250 Camberwell Road,
Camberwell, Victoria 3124, Australia (a division of Pearson Australia Group Pty Ltd);
Penguin Books India Pvt Ltd, 11 Community Centre, Panchsheel Park, New Delhi -
110 017, India; Penguin Group (NZ), Cnr Airborne and Rosedale Roads, Albany, Auckland,
New Zealand (a division of Pearson New Zealand Ltd); Penguin Books
(South Africa) (Pty) Ltd, 24 Sturdee Avenue, Rosebank, Johannesburg 2196, South Africa

Penguin Books Ltd, Registered Offices: 80 Strand, London WC2R 0RL, England

Published by Gotham Books, a division of Penguin Group (USA) Inc.
Previously published as a Gotham Books hardcover edition.

First trade paperback printing, April 2005
10 9 8 7 6

Copyright © 2004 by Jody Vasquez
All rights reserved

Gotham Books and the skyscraper logo are trademarks of Penguin Group (USA) Inc.

THE LIBRARY OF CONGRESS HAS CATALOGED THE
GOTHAM BOOKS HARDCOVER EDITION AS FOLLOWS:
Vasquez, Jody.
Afternoons with Mr. Hogan : a boy, a golf legend, and the lessons
of a lifetime / by Jody Vasquez.
p. cm.
ISBN 1-592-40051-5 (hardcover : alk. paper) 1-592-40113-9 (pbk.)
1. Hogan, Ben, 1912—Anecdotes.   2. Vasquez, Jody.   3. Golfers—United States—
Biography—Anecdotes.   I. Title.
GV964.H6V37   2004
796.352'092—dc22

Printed in the United States of America
Set in Centaur MT   Designed by Sabrina Bowers

CONTENTS

INTRODUCTION

STORIES ABOUT THE GREAT Ben Hogan have become a stand-alone category in golf. There are hundreds of tales and anecdotes, most relating to some aspect of his unique personality, legendary work ethic, strong character and sheer genius as a golfer. Hogan stories invariably carry a delicious punch line that leaves the listener laughing, shaking their head in disbelief or simply quiet, struck with reverential awe. Hogan stories age well and are as relevant today as ever. They are rarely apocryphal, though many have become distorted in the thousandth retelling. The stories are a casualty of being passed from one person to the next, over the course of many years.

My stories about Mr. Hogan are personal and are the subject of this book. In the spring of 1964, when I was 17 years old, I began shagging balls for Mr. Hogan during his long, frequent practice sessions at Shady Oaks Country Club in Fort Worth, Texas. Out of this experience came a relationship that continued, with some interruption, until his death in 1997. Whereas most books about Mr. Hogan have been written by people who observed him from a distance, the experiences I relate were gathered firsthand.

When someone discovers that I knew Mr. Hogan, an endless string of questions ensues. Was he as aloof as people say? Did he really practice for hours on end? What did he have to say about the golf swing? Were his clubs as unusual as we've been told? After answering so many Hogan questions through the years and telling and retelling so many of my favorite Hogan stories, I decided to commit these stories to paper.

This is not an exhaustive recounting of Mr. Hogan's life. Biographies of Mr. Hogan have been done before, and in truth, few facts about his personal history came to light during our association. This book is not instructional either, though some of the more interesting things Mr. Hogan had to say about the golf swing—including his famed swing secret—I think are fascinating, and merit revelation. Nor is this book a vain attempt to break down his mystique. The quasi-psychology stuff isn't my cup of tea.

My purpose is simply to reveal the same stories I have been telling people for many years. To this day I never tire of telling them. One of my dearest friends, Dale Hansen, and I, on our first meeting, began discussing Mr. Hogan one late afternoon and ended up closing the club bar at five o'clock the following morning. The more Hogan stories the better, I say.

I knew Mr. Hogan in a variety of settings. He had four distinct parts to his life: family, golf, business and social. Each was compartmentalized. If you were social with Mr. Hogan, you knew him socially only. He didn't talk business within that setting and he certainly didn't discuss golf. By the same token, he kept business matters with his business associates and golf matters with a carefully chosen few or only to himself. As surprising as it may seem, his wife, Valerie, knew very little about his golf life inside the ropes and practically nothing about his business side. When visiting with Mrs. Hogan one afternoon, I mentioned that Mr. Hogan had passed on his swing secret to me years before. She told me she didn't doubt it at all, but I could tell in her eyes she had no clue what it was. I never told her.

Because of the length of time I spent with him and the circumstances under which I knew him, I was lucky enough to cross the boundaries of all these areas. I saw his social interactions with his friends and acquaintances at Shady Oaks, where he was most relaxed. In later years, through knowing his associates at the Ben Hogan Company, I gained knowledge of his approach to business. And through the course of shagging balls for him, I gathered insight into his existence as a golfer that few others experienced. Finally, by observing his interaction with his family, I gained a unique perspective on his character and values.

I was not a close or personal friend of Mr. Hogan. While he and Mrs. Hogan were exceedingly generous to me, I never counted them among my intimate friends. In the end we simply shared some moments in time, the result of which was an association and mutual respect that, for me, has lasted a lifetime.

When Mr. Hogan passed away, I sometimes found myself wishing I had asked him more penetrating questions.

Reflecting more on that, I realized how fearful I always was of being too intrusive. In a way I still am. On balance, however, I am revealing nothing that would upset the Hogans. This especially applies to my decision to reveal his famous swing secret. My feeling is that, if he didn't want anyone to know about it, he wouldn't have shared it with me to begin with. I have a feeling he knew I would one day discuss it freely with others, and perhaps even write about it. I'm very happy and proud to discuss it openly here.

In addition to giving the golfing public further insight into Mr. Hogan's golf game, I have a couple of other reasons for writing this book. After meeting someone who then finds out about my Hogan connection, I am often regaled with their own Hogan story. More times than I can count, I realize it's a story that has come full circle—it's a story I had told someone else that had passed through several renditions and come back to me largely changed. This book is a good way to at least set down all *my* Hogan stories accurately.

Also, I feel compelled to share these stories because I feel they possess a certain historical value. I don't want them to die. As friends and competitors of Mr. Hogan pass on, so do the stories. In preserving these stories, we are pulling back the curtain on Mr. Hogan for future generations. This applies especially to my three sons, who have always enjoyed hearing me discuss Mr. Hogan. One day, I think it'd be nice for their children to know these stories.

Ben Hogan was a great golfer. I believe he was an even better person. He was as dedicated to his work as anyone I have ever met. By hitting thousands of balls and digging his secret out of the dirt, he achieved a wonderful insight into playing golf and in pursuing perfection in life. I hope that by sharing some of the insight he shared with me, I am continuing his legacy.

JODY VASQUEZ
FORT WORTH, TEXAS
JUNE 2003

AFTERNOONS WITH
MR. HOGAN

Price of Admission:
95 Cents an Hour

FORT WORTH HAS PRODUCED some interesting and dynamic individuals, but its most widely revered and well-known citizen was Ben Hogan. Despite his prominence in my hometown while I was growing up, I wasn't very familiar with the legendary golfer. That was about to change.

I was 17 years old and attending Northside High School when an ordinary question changed my life. I was enjoying an uneventful spring morning in Mrs. Johnston's geometry class, when a classmate, Gary Lumpkin, leaned across the aisle and asked me if I needed a job for the summer. Since I didn't have a job lined up yet, I was all ears.

I played on the school golf team, so he knew I'd love what he was about to say. He told me there was a job opening in the golf shop at Shady Oaks Country Club. Actually, the job was Gary's. He was leaving town after the spring semester to rejoin his parents. His dad was in the Air Force and was heading back home to Chicago. I jumped at the chance. I thought working in a golf shop at a country club like Shady Oaks would be a perfect way to spend my summer. It certainly would beat my other option, sacking groceries at Hill's Grocery Store on Twenty-fifth Street.

On Saturday, Gary took me to Shady Oaks to meet with Art Hall, the golf professional. The job as Art described it was simple: I would start each morning at 7:30, set up the driving range, and then take care of the members when they began arriving a short time later. It's the same bag-room job you see kids handling at just about any course you might play. I would clean their golf clubs, pick up the driving range balls, vacuum the shop floors, and perform other odd tasks. Art eventually offered me the position, and I eagerly accepted it.

At the time, Mr. Hogan practiced almost every weekday afternoon at Shady Oaks. He didn't hit balls on the driving range with the general membership. Instead he hired caddies to go out on the course with him to his private practice areas. There he would hit his own balls for a few hours and the caddies would pick them up. A variety of caddies might get the call to work for Mr. Hogan, although he did have a semi-regular caddie in Fort Worth. Known only as "Old Folks," he was on Hogan's bag when he played casually with friends or was competing in the Colonial National Invitation Tournament. Old Folks was an easygoing big black guy who worked for the local telephone company and came to the course when Mr. Hogan needed someone to work his bag. But at Shady Oaks, no individual worked exclusively for Mr. Hogan as a shag-boy until I began working for him in 1964.

I should make clear that I did not caddie for Mr. Hogan. Although I spent countless hours shagging balls for him,

I never caddied for him on the course. When Mr. Hogan played, he usually walked using Old Folks or one of the local caddies. Sometimes a college kid from Texas Christian University would get his bag. That must have been a real treat. You show up expecting to chase balls for a 15-handicapper and bingo, there's Ben Hogan's bag instead. If no caddies were available, Mr. Hogan would put his bag on a cart like everybody else.

After the Shady noontime crowd had teed off and was on the course, there wasn't much to do in the golf shop. The entire shop staff consisted of the head pro, Art; his two assistants, Tom Sisolak and Fred Chancey; and me. Shady Oaks didn't need a big staff because the club had only about 100-plus members. Therefore, my working for Mr. Hogan on a regular basis made sense. As I was always at the club, Art didn't have to scramble around on busy days looking for someone to accompany Mr. Hogan. It wasn't fair to ask a caddie who was there to make money carrying someone's bag to hang around and see what Mr. Hogan was going to do. Moreover, my working for Mr. Hogan saved Art from paying me my usual wage of 95 cents an hour for working in the shop. To me, the most sensible aspect was the fact Mr. Hogan paid much better than Art did.

I enjoyed my job with Mr. Hogan from the start. It was pretty exciting just sitting next to him on a cart waiting to hear what he might say, even though he didn't say anything to me at first. It's not often a teenager gets to stand in the shadow of an icon and witness firsthand the countless things others would have paid to see but couldn't. At first, I didn't know enough about Mr. Hogan to appreciate his legendary accomplishments, but I was quickly schooled in all things Hogan, beginning with his reason for choosing Shady Oaks as a place to practice and hang his hat. A private club, Shady Oaks was built by Marvin Leonard in 1959. Mr. Marvin, as he was affectionately known, was an exceptional individual and Mr. Hogan's best friend. Prior to building Shady Oaks, Mr. Leonard was best known for building Colonial Country Club, also in Fort Worth. Colonial is recognized as the best golf course in Texas and is regularly ranked among the top 50 best courses in America. Opened in 1936, Colonial established the prestigious Colonial National Invitation Tournament in 1946. It helped that Hogan won the event a record five times; for decades it has been known as "Hogan's Alley," and is an official stop on the PGA Tour.

Colonial was Mr. Hogan's second home until Mr. Marvin opened Shady Oaks. At that time, Mr. Hogan and a small group of invited friends moved to play at the new course, which is located on the west side of Fort Worth. Even though Mr. Hogan spent all his time at Shady Oaks and visited Colonial only on special occasions, Colonial remained his home course in his heart. When he referred to his "home club," he was referring to Colonial.

The first story I remember being told about Mr. Hogan was of his 1949 Greyhound bus accident. It's one of the most inspiring stories in sports history, but it wasn't until I visited with Mrs. Hogan in 1994 that I fully understood the extent of what Mr. Hogan had gone through. I was awed, and still am, by his determination to rise up and return to the game. The level of accomplishment he achieved after all he had endured is something else entirely. I couldn't have done it. I doubt many could. I think after you read a little more, the PGA Tour's Ben Hogan Award given annually to honor a recovering player may hold a deeper meaning for you.

Mr. Hogan's reputation for privacy and his standoffish demeanor resulted in little interaction between him and the Shady Oaks membership in general. While I worked at Shady, it was unofficial policy that everyone leave him alone, especially when he sat at his special table in a corner of the men's grill. The table, which is reserved for him to this day, is large and round and easily seats six people. But, Mr. Hogan always sat alone. He would drink his glass of Chardonnay, eat lunch, and sometimes finish his meal with a slice of apple pie with cheddar cheese melted on top (his and Mr. Marvin's favorite dessert). When someone did approach him at his table, he would say hello and quickly move away. It was rare for someone to pull up a chair and sit to visit with him. Despite this, members loved to walk over and introduce their guests to Mr. Hogan. Introductions would be made and handshakes exchanged. There was very little small talk. The awkwardness was pronounced; people didn't know what to talk about with Mr. Hogan. What would you say to him? To make matters even tougher, he was uncomfortable talking with people he didn't know well. Even after shagging balls for him for years, we more often than not rode out and back to the practice area without exchanging a word. A quick hello and that might very well be it for the day. When he came to Shady, he came for a purpose and not simply to kill time.

At Shady Oaks, Mr. Hogan preferred practicing to playing. When he did play, typically, it was in a noon game with the "gangsome." The gangsome was a group of ten to fifteen guys who played for some pretty big money by those days' standards. They were all pretty well-heeled and openly enjoyed the thrill of betting. The group included Mr. Hogan's brother, Royal (one of the better players), a cast of characters from oilmen to corporate types, and Mr. Marvin, who not only built the club but also owned it up until 1970 when he sold it to the Shady membership. Generally, these guys were medium- to high-handicap players who loved the action.

The gangsome always tried to talk Mr. Hogan into playing with them, but more often than not he turned them down. He played with them on occasion, however, and when he did the foursome group pairings were done randomly. When Tom Sisolak went to the grill to find out who was playing, generally, he was told to team Mr. Hogan with somebody. Tom chose the players randomly, though occasionally someone would speak up for the honor of joining his group. Sometimes, Mr. Hogan and a partner of his choosing would take the "swing" that day.

The swing was a fascinating game and a complicated one. Two players were chosen to play against all combinations of the other players who showed up to play that day. One memorable Friday, Mr. Hogan was a swing partner with Earl Baldridge, president of Champlin Oil Company. Baldridge was an 18-handicapper, and not a very good one at that. They lost, and the financial implication was so significant that Mr. Hogan demanded that he and Baldridge team up again the next day—with the condition that all bets be doubled. The gang was more than happy to oblige.

A rumor still persists that Mr. Hogan had a private chat with Henry Martin, the course superintendent, before leaving the club that evening. Mr. Hogan is said to have asked Henry to set Saturday's pins in places that were especially challenging. On the first hole, for example, the hole was cut on a steep slope at the very front of the green. If you hit your approach shot above the pin, it was impossible to two-putt. The stage was set. When the players finished their rounds that Saturday and walked into the grill, the first thing they saw was Mr. Hogan's hat turned upside down in the middle of his table. The Hogan/Baldridge team killed everybody. Mr. Hogan shot 62, and Baldridge filled in the gaps. Although I wasn't there to see the money flutter into the cap that day, I was told it amounted to approximately $20,000.

From that, it's easy to understand why Mr. Hogan and the entire gang took this noon game seriously. They even employed their own handicap system. Sisolak would refigure all the players' scores after every round. He kept a book especially for it. Tom would recalculate the scoring average of the last 15 rounds played and compute a current handicap. The USGA handicap system was ignored by the gangsome. The money was serious enough that the gang wanted up-to-the-minute handicaps, computed using *all* scores. They watched one another like hawks. Sandbagging was never an issue, though it hardly would have mattered to Mr. Hogan. One of the curious things about him was, he hated to give handicap strokes when involved in an individual player-to-player bet. He had to spot the gangsome types something, of course, because those were team bets, but if you played Mr. Hogan head-to-head, you played him straight up. One would think he would have difficulty getting a game this way, but I suspect many amateurs thought losing a small bet to Ben Hogan a small price to pay for the great privilege of playing with him.

Timing is everything in life. When I first started working at Shady, Mr. Hogan was 51 years old and at the end of his playing career. He didn't play in formal competition much, which enabled him to spend more time at Shady Oaks and consequently, for me to get to know him. There was no Champions Tour (not that he would have played on it anyway); yet, he still was deeply committed to being a competitive golfer. He maintained a desire to win and felt he could still compete even though his last victory had been at the Colonial in 1959. While I was shagging for him, he still had flashes of his old self like the back nine round he shot at the Masters in '67.

Mr. Hogan grew to know me, which would have been highly unlikely had he traveled the PGA Tour steadily. Maybe because I met him later in life, I never saw the hard side of his character that people talk about. I don't believe he was cold or unfeeling. My first impression of Mr. Hogan was how confidently he carried himself. He seemed so strong, positive and controlled. I couldn't imagine that anything could ever rattle him. His voice was strong and confident, his tone deep and commanding. Even the way he used his hands while talking spoke volumes to the inner confidence he exuded. With that, I thought he was charismatic and charming—and still somewhat curmudgeonly. I doubt I will ever again meet an individual as positive about his place in life as Mr. Hogan was. I'm sure he was not always that way, but when I was around him he clearly knew exactly who he was and he never strayed from that. If you've ever been fortunate enough to watch a hawk in flight or see it moving toward its prey, you would fully understand why he carried his nickname: the Hawk.

In the fall of 1968, I resigned from my job at Shady Oaks and went to work at another club in Arlington, Texas, where I attended college. Moving to that new job closed the ball-shagging chapter in my life and my regular contact with Mr. Hogan. Nevertheless, in the years that followed until his death in 1997, I was lucky enough to remain in contact with him and feel very privileged to have spent quality time visiting with him.

Like I said, timing *is* everything. I came to Shady Oaks when I was young enough to accept working for 95 cents an hour and not feel I was underpaid. If this or any other circumstance were different, the most extraordinary relationship of my life would never have taken place.

2

Practice as an Art Form

IN SPORTS THERE ARE ATHLETES who have set records that will never be broken. In baseball, you think of Cal Ripken, Jr.'s 2,632 consecutive games played. In basketball, it's Wilt Chamberlain's single-game scoring record of 100 points. In golf, it's Byron Nelson's string of 11 consecutive PGA Tour victories in 1945.

But the record book doesn't tell everything. There is a select group of athletes who didn't just shatter records to mark their place in history, but must be classified as great because they went beyond the record books and actually altered the fundamental nature of the sport they played. A classic example is Bob Hayes, who won the gold medal in the 100-meter dash at the 1964 Olympic Games. He was known as the fastest human in the world ... *Bullet Bob Hayes.* Then, he became a wide receiver for the Dallas Cowboys. Hayes' speed was so overwhelming that man-to-man defensive coverages simply couldn't contain him. The zone defense was invented purely because of him. Today, zone defenses are the norm. The NBA's Chamberlain was great by any measure, but his dominance was such that the league was forced to widen the free-throw lane near the basket to give smaller foes a fighting chance.

In golf, the person who had such a strategy-altering impact was Ben Hogan. His relentless work on the practice tee can be linked directly with his success and a level of performance that didn't exist in his era or before. Others were forced to follow his lead or else be left behind. He was the first player to make practice a basic part of the game, not just before a tournament but during it.

Until Mr. Hogan came along, most players didn't feel the need or inclination to practice seriously. Practice was a warm-up routine prior to the day's play. Mr. Hogan didn't agree with them. He often said that if he missed a shot during play, he catalogued it in his mind. Once finished with his round, he moved directly to the practice tee to work on that missed shot. By practicing the missed shot time and time again, he ensured that he didn't make the same mistake twice.

Raymond Gafford, a legendary club pro in Fort Worth, played in several PGA Tour events during the Hogan era. A story he told me clearly illustrates the view held by players of that era. Raymond was near the lead in a Chicago-area tour event in the early 1950s. He was paired with Bob (Rossy) Rosburg, who later won the 1959 PGA Championship. Both players struggled but had managed to stay close to the lead. Raymond knew it was going to be a pretty big payday if he could just work out a few kinks in his swing. So he suggested to Rossy that the two of them should go to the practice tee after lunch and help each other with their swings.

Rossy's reply was simple: "Why would I want to go to the practice tee and practice this?" With that, he made a low cut-shot motion with his right hand, while extending his arm out to indicate a shot fading down the right side of the fairway. You can see what practicing meant to that generation of players.

Mr. Hogan held a contrary view. He felt everyone would benefit from lots of practice. One of the few times he spoke out against his competitors was in a radio interview during an event in which he and Byron Nelson were competing. He made an off-the-cuff comment that Nelson would have done better if he and the rest of the field would spend more time hitting balls on the practice tee and less time elsewhere.

Mr. Hogan's influence is evident today. Instructors stress to their pupils the importance of practice. Fans and sportswriters are quick to criticize the work ethic of a pro who doesn't work hard enough. You may not see many players on the practice tee until dark on Saturday night, but on their weeks away from tournament golf they spend many hours that go unnoticed.

As Mr. Hogan's reputation grew, his practice sessions became renowned. From Jack Nicklaus to tour caddies, everyone wanted to watch the legend at work. I have often heard well-known instructors lament that they never saw Mr. Hogan hit a shot in person and only have video as a frame of reference. That's too bad. It was a different game when you saw it live.

Mr. Hogan was dedicated to practice from the very beginning. It was his nature. The first practice story I ever heard about him came from Aneila Goldthwaite, an excellent player in her day who had been a member of Shady Oaks and Rivercrest. Her husband, Frank, held the area Toro dealership, which sold golf course maintenance equipment and also distributed Wilson golf equipment.

Mrs. Goldthwaite told me she first knew Mr. Hogan when he was caddying at Rivercrest in his younger days. Because of his interest in golf, she gave him a dozen brand-new Wilson golf balls and a pitching wedge. She handed them to him early one morning before she went out to play. Mr. Hogan was there to caddy, but instead he immediately went to an area on the grounds and started hitting the balls. She went out to play, had lunch and when she left to go home, he was still practicing. Later that evening, she and Frank returned to the club for dinner and, sure enough, young Ben Hogan was still there hitting balls.

A month or so went by. One morning, Mr. Hogan visited her at the Toro office. She greeted him by asking, "Ben, what can I do for you?" He answered, "I was wondering if I might have another box of Wilson golf balls." Her response was, "You've lost them already?" To which he emphatically replied, "No," and handed her the box with the entire dozen still in it. She opened the box and could hardly believe what she saw. The golf ball covers were so worn that the dimples were almost smooth. There weren't any cuts or creases; Mr. Hogan had simply worn them out.

Mrs. Goldthwaite was shocked, especially because it had been such a short time since she had given them to him. What did she do next or how did she respond? She gave him another dozen and told him to come back when those were worn out. She didn't say if Mr. Hogan ever asked for another pitching wedge.

A METHOD TO THE MADNESS

MR. HOGAN LOVED TO PRACTICE, but never hit balls on the practice range. Even when he went out to play he'd only hit a couple of shots to loosen up, but nothing more serious. He didn't believe in merely hitting balls to a wide, ill-defined area. He believed that hitting to a specific target imposed a bit of pressure and intensified your sense of purpose. Driving ranges today are more refined than they were 40 years ago; there are flagsticks, yardage markers and makeshift greens to hit to. The range at Shady Oaks was a wide-open expanse. That's one reason he preferred practicing in areas out on the course itself.

Given a nice practice facility, I still doubt he would have spent much time there. Mr. Hogan enjoyed practicing alone, out on the course. He didn't want anybody around. Seldom, if ever, did he allow anyone to sit or stand within sight. He wasn't social during that part of his day. The members played through as he hit across fairways. Sometimes they waved, but rarely did they stop over to chat, and they never sat and watched. Everyone knew he did not like being distracted. On occasion he and I might chat while driving out and sometimes coming back in, but once we arrived at the practice spot, nothing was said. It was time to work.

Another reason he liked the course was that he preferred hitting his own balls. The driving-range balls were (and still are) rock hard and designed more for durability than performance. The quality of the golf ball was paramount with Mr. Hogan. He believed that if the quality of the ball was poor, it was impossible to glean anything about his swing based on the flight of the ball. The golf ball in flight doesn't lie—if it's a quality ball. It's been related that Mr. Hogan checked his golf balls before he played to make sure the paint was consistent in depth across the entire surface. It's true; he confirmed it to me. I don't think he thought other players did the same or much less cared.

The most critical reason Mr. Hogan avoided the range, however, was wind direction. He always hit balls with the wind blowing right to left as he stood over the ball. He wanted the wind hitting him in the chest. That way, even if the wind was blowing hard, he didn't have to worry about losing his balance during the swing and could concentrate on other things. To that end, he used two primary areas for practicing, both on Shady Oaks' back nine. His main area was to the right—or northeast—of the 11th green. This positioning gave him a southwesterly wind to play into. If the wind was from the north, we moved over to an area between the 17th tee and the 18th fairway.

When he was not playing in a PGA event, Mr. Hogan rarely did anything golf-related on Saturday, though sometimes he would play 18 holes with the Saturday gangsome. Never once did he play or practice on Sunday.

To start a session, I loaded Mr. Hogan's golf bag on a

golf cart and waited for him to come out of the locker room. By the time he walked through the golf shop door, he had already decided where he wanted to practice that day and drove us to his spot. The routine would begin.

He would get out of the cart and start inspecting the ground. He was selective and deliberate about finding just the right spot to use. Once he found a good place from which to play, he pointed with his finger to the spot he wanted without saying a word. I'd dump the balls onto the ground and head out.

Caddies have different techniques for shagging balls. Some catch the ball in the air baseball-style before it hits the ground, sometimes using a glove or a towel. With Mr. Hogan that would have been easy because he was so accurate, it would've been like playing catch with him. I never did that. For one, I enjoyed watching how far each shot spun back after it landed—such was the degree to which he could control the spin of the ball. Generally, he spun the ball furiously on his full swings, yet, he also would dead-arm shots to reduce spin. I could tell what he was working on just by watching the ball land and spin. His sense of feel was marvelous.

As each ball came to rest, I retrieved it and always wiped it with a wet towel before tossing it in his shag bag. When the balls hit the ground, they either got grass stains or mud on them. Mr. Hogan did not hit dirty balls, so I made sure I carefully cleaned each one.

Like many golfers, Mr. Hogan started his practice session with his sand wedge and then progressed through the set. He never quit his session until he worked his way through the entire bag. The driver was always the last club he hit. I don't recall that he ever counted balls in such a way that he hit 10 or 12 balls with his 9-iron before he moved on. His sessions were fully results-oriented. I never had the impression that he hit balls only to kill a few more minutes before heading back. Every swing had its purpose.

Mr. Hogan would hit the first bag, which contained roughly 100 balls, moving through the clubs in a normal progression—9, 8, 7, and so on. There was nothing unusual about the speed with which he progressed through a bag of balls. He would hit a ball, watch until it landed and then move to the next one. I didn't pay much attention to his body motion or try to glean a swing tip as he struck his shots. I was focused elsewhere, like on not getting hit by the ball. You may laugh, but that was a real possibility.

After he finished hitting the last ball in the first bag, he would walk over to the cart and light a cigarette. He sat on the edge of the cart seat and waited for me to come in. He never waved me in or called out to me. If he lit a cigarette, it meant he was out of balls.

The first couple of sessions I ran in as fast as I could, thinking it might impress him. Eventually I realized that the time between bags was Mr. Hogan's downtime. So I took my time walking in to give him time to finish his cigarette. When I finally reached him, he would stand up, look around and point to a new spot. I would dump out the balls and then head back out to my spot. We seldom spoke to each other.

I have a couple of friends who followed me in shagging for Mr. Hogan. When we see each other at a social function instead of saying hello, we'll walk up to each other and simply point our right index finger at the ground. We get some weird looks from those standing around us. It's good for a laugh! After all, there aren't many members of this club.

Normally, Mr. Hogan would start hitting shots before I returned to the landing area. After hitting the first bag of balls, he had usually worked his way up to the longer irons, so I had farther to run. I didn't want to get behind picking up the balls he'd already hit, so I retrieved them quickly. I cleaned them off and dropped them in the bag. Getting behind with Mr. Hogan still hitting shots at you was dangerous. He kept hitting more balls whether you were caught up or not. And, since the balls are coming straight at you, and believe me they were, you had to find each ball in flight so you could move and not get hit.

The shots that missed me but found their way directly into the bag were also cause for concern. Mr. Hogan hit lots of balls that went straight in the bag, which was amazing and great fun to watch. Some flew straight in and some would land and hop in. Either way, it got your attention. However, I would quickly pore through the bag for the ball with a grass or mud stain on it so I could clean it. It was nerve-wracking because balls that only struck the ground once were difficult to locate. The danger element added to the hassle: As I scrambled to find the ball, Mr. Hogan was getting ready or already hitting another one and I didn't want to take my eyes off the next one coming at me. The shorter the club he was hitting, the more intense was my search for the dirty ball.

I saw an old video of him practicing for the 1964 PGA in

Ohio and what caught my eye was how the caddy shagging for him kept moving around from one spot to another as Mr. Hogan hit. Instantly, I thought, he's doing that on purpose. Mr. Hogan was afraid he'd hit the guy if he hit straight at him, probably would have.

That, in fact, was the most difficult part of my job—making sure his golf ball didn't hit me. I never allowed myself to get distracted while he was hitting. We each had our unspoken role in how the practice session worked: Mr. Hogan's objective was to hit me and mine was to make sure he didn't. I catch myself joking about it, but it wasn't funny at the time. He was so accurate. Usually, when we were out and I'd almost get hit, I'd think, "Wow, I got lucky again." I kept wondering when my day would come. I had some anxious moments as I stood there diligently looking up into the sky and straining to find the golf ball that he'd hit. In my heart of hearts, I *knew* it was coming at me. Over time I even found myself jokingly checking the weather report, especially to find out what type of sky we would have. I always hated a "high sky," one without clouds. I couldn't afford sunglasses. I only made 95 cents an hour for goodness sake, so the days with no clouds were murder.

Amazingly enough, after hitting thousands upon thousands of golf balls in my direction, he never once hit me. I don't know what it felt like to be hit by one of Mr. Hogan's shots, but I know exactly what a golf ball sounds like as it passes by your ear! The ball makes a bee-like, zinging sound and then you have this "wow" feeling just after it goes by you.

There are certain experiences you never forget, and the sound of a golf ball spinning by my head is one that is cemented in my memory.

The end of a practice session was usually uneventful. Mr. Hogan would wave me to trot in and I'd gather the balls he didn't hit. Meanwhile, Mr. Hogan lit another cigarette. Then we'd get in the cart and make the 10-minute ride back to the clubhouse. Usually we drove in silence. Sometimes we would stop and he would do some chipping and putting.

Those 10-minute rides turned out to be some of the most valuable time I spent with him. This was when he shared most of the thoughts I've written into these pages. When he felt like talking or had something on his mind, he would share it as though I was his closest friend. He never talked down to me or made me feel like a little kid. If I asked him to explain himself, he did so seriously and at length. It was as though he was telling me something that would last a lifetime. It has.

THE FIRST TIME WAS A CHARM

WHEN I REFLECT on the many times I shagged balls for Mr. Hogan, my very first practice session stands out in my mind and remains a great source of humor for me. One day after I had been working in the shop for a few weeks, Art Hall couldn't find anybody to go out and shag balls for Mr. Hogan. All the caddies were on the course with other players. It was either Art or me, and Art opted for me.

I had no idea what to expect. I loaded Mr. Hogan's golf bag on a golf cart, sat down and nervously waited for him. When he came through the golf shop door he didn't say a word to me. He sat down in the cart and off we went. We rode in silence to his spot by the 11th green, which I soon discovered was his favorite practice area. When we arrived, Mr. Hogan got out of the cart and scoured the ground. I remember saying to myself, "What the heck is he looking for?" You should remember I was 17 and a little green under the collar.

Next, he pointed his right index finger toward the ground at a spot a few yards in front of the cart. I quickly got out of the cart with his bag of balls, opened the bag, and spilled the balls on the spot where he had pointed. All this time, he never looked over toward me. It was silent instruction. Luckily, I guessed his meaning correctly and survived the first test.

Not really knowing what to expect next, I trotted out a few yards. I knew he was going to hit balls, but I didn't know exactly where or how far. While I was running out, he walked over to his bag and took out a club. I ran out about 50 yards and looked back. I saw him starting to hit his first shot. It was a soft wedge in the general area I had reached. I walked over, picked up the ball and wiped the grass stain off it with my wet towel, just like Art had told me to do. I dropped the ball into the bag at my feet. Mr. Hogan hit his next shot in the same area. I decided this was the spot he wanted to hit his shots, so I left the bag there and moved off to the side some five to seven yards.

The next shot was right at me. I walked over and picked up the bag. I moved it over to where I had been standing and repositioned myself a few yards off to the side. Again, the next shot was right at me! I walked over, grabbed the bag and moved it again. When I looked up, Mr. Hogan was standing there leaning on his club and staring out at me. He must have thought I was attempting to do my best Charlie Chaplin impression. Then he waved for me to come in.

At first I thought he was cutting the session short. But when I stopped in front of him to pick up the un-hit balls, he looked at me and spoke for the first time. "Son, keep the bag with you. I'm going to hit the balls at you no matter where you stand or put that bag. It would be easier on the both of us if you didn't have to move around to find the bag so you can put the balls in it."

Until that moment, the idea that he purposely wanted to hit his shots at me hadn't occurred to me. I muttered a polite, "Yes sir," and ran back out to my spot. From then on, I always kept the bag at my feet—and I relayed that information to the guys after me to do the same. Mr. Hogan was right, of course. Hitting right at me was easier for both of us, me especially. Generally, all I had to do was bend over, pick up the ball at my feet and clean it off after he hit it at me. Okay . . . with the driver I had to take a couple of steps before I bent over to pick the thing up.

Oh yes, his final comment to me before I ran back out was, ". . . and pay attention." Think maybe he had hit somebody before?

LOOKING OUT FOR NO. 1

ONE DAY, as we were riding in from an afternoon practice session, I remarked that he had hit more sand wedge shots than he normally did. His comment was that he couldn't get comfortable hitting the shots he wanted to hit with his sand wedge so he simply kept hitting it. Mr. Hogan told me that he never moved from one club to the next until he felt he was perfect with the club resting in his hands. It didn't matter what club he was hitting. If he was hitting a 7-iron and hadn't attained full trust in the shots he hit with that club, he'd practice with it until he did. I innocently joked that if I applied that standard, I'd never get past hitting my sand wedge. In typical Hogan fashion, he looked dead at me and asked, *"Why would you want to?"*

The truth in that statement is immutable. To me, what Mr. Hogan said that day ranks second in importance only to the revelation of his swing secret. It speaks to the principle of commitment, which I try to apply to everything I do. As Mr. Hogan saw it, you either did things right or didn't do them at all. He believed that what other people thought of you was secondary or didn't matter, but what you thought of yourself and your dedication to succeed was more important. If it were necessary to hit only his sand wedge for ten consecutive practice sessions, Mr. Hogan would have done it without hesitation and without regard for what others thought.

Ben Hogan never tried to please you, Mrs. Hogan, fellow players or the media. He was in it for himself. The bottom line: To be successful at the highest level of anything, you have to be selfish.

MIXING IT UP

WHENEVER MR. HOGAN was going to play somewhere, his shotmaking in practice took on a specific pattern. He would start off by hitting normal shots with his sand wedge, but when he went to the 9-iron he began mixing up his shots in a regimented fashion. The first ball he hit was straight. The next one was a fade. The third one was a draw. He would repeat this cycle—straight shot, fade, draw—over and over. He did this from the 9-iron through the driver.

When Mr. Hogan had finished hitting his first full bag of balls, I would walk in and ask him what tournament he was getting ready for. He would just look at me and smile. He would never say which one. I'd trot back out, and we'd pick up where he'd left off. These sessions usually lasted more than two hours.

I always was puzzled by his reluctance to reveal what tournament he was getting ready for. Who was I gonna tell? Moreover, I was awed by this shotmaking procedure, which you may want to try sometime. The concentration it requires is considerable; I personally felt I was losing my mind after 15 minutes, which seemed like an eternity. First of all, a pretty high level of frustration sets in. Second, you can't hit the pattern without missing a shot in the routine. We're not that good. Mr. Hogan was.

THE SOUND OF MUSIC

IT'S TRUE WHAT EVERYONE SAYS about watching Mr. Hogan practice: It was pure pleasure. His shots were so crisp, the motion of his swing so fluid. His balance was perfect on every swing. Have you ever seen a picture of Hogan swinging a club off-balance like Arnold Palmer or one-handed like Tiger Woods? I never tired of watching and listening.

Yes, listening. The sound of Mr. Hogan's club striking the ball was distinctive. It was a deep, low-pitched sound that seemed heavy. It was never tinny. The sound also hung in the air a while. It reverberated, as though the ball was in contact with the clubface for an inordinately long time. Every shot he hit had that quality. I believe his flat swing plane enabled him to keep the clubhead traveling along the target line longer, and thus kept the ball on the clubface an instant longer. Hence, the deliciously unique sound.

I've heard that sound only one other time. I've been on Colonial's PGA Tour Tournament committee for many years, and my job is to manage the practice range that week. One day back in the mid '90s, I was standing on the practice tee with my back to the PGA Tour players who were hitting. I was talking to someone when I was distracted by a familiar sound. I stood there for a minute without turning around and listened more intently. I heard the sound again.

When I looked over my shoulder, there was Hal Sutton hitting iron shots right behind me. I never said anything about it to Hal, but it's the only time in all my years of playing golf and hearing shots come off a clubface that I've ever heard the ball sound the same as Mr. Hogan's. It must say something, I think, about Hal Sutton's ability to compress the ball.

A SAD HIATUS

I BEGAN SHAGGING BALLS for Mr. Hogan 15 years after the famous 1949 Greyhound bus accident. The effect on his legs—his left leg in particular—is well known. But only a couple of people know of the profound effect the accident had on his shoulders. In fact, if you look at a photograph of Mr. Hogan in his hospital bed, it's clear he was a mess from head to toe.

One day, Mr. Hogan told me this was going to be his last day of practicing for a couple of months. Naturally, I asked why. Mr. Hogan took my hand and placed it on his shoulder just at the top of his collarbone. It's the point off your shoulder where the collarbone moves toward the front of your body. You can feel a gap right at the base of your neck. There's this split before you touch your neck. This spot is the acromioclavicular joint (ACJ), which lies over the top of the shoulder. The ACJ is the gliding joint that forms the connection between the acromion of the shoulder blade (scapula) and the collarbone (clavicle). It allows the shoulder to rise and fall (shrug) and helps stabilize the shoulder joint.

He had a huge calcium deposit protruding there, as if the top half of a golf ball was sitting under his shirt. He had them on both shoulders. In the bus accident, he had injured both his shoulders. Since the accident, the deposits had continued to grow to the point where he could no longer stand the pain. He had never complained about it, so I was caught totally off guard.

Mr. Hogan went to New Orleans to a doctor who scraped the deposits off. Mr. Hogan had them both done at the same time. For several weeks after the surgery, he walked around with both arms in slings. Eventually the slings were discarded and Mr. Hogan began putting a bit, and then chipping. Finally, in the fall, he was ready to hit full shots, which he hadn't done in quite some time.

I remember this session vividly. We were at his practice area over by the 17th tee. Mr. Hogan's very first swing was with his sand wedge and it was textbook, as if he hadn't missed any practice at all. But, he bladed the next shot. I still remember my feeling of shock. I'd never seen him blade a shot before, which gave me the impression that his first swing must have hurt him a bit. He kept at it with the sand wedge for two hours, and to me the shots looked like the same old Ben Hogan. As the week passed, he moved up slowly from one club to the next.

Then came the afternoon he moved to his fairway woods. I knew this would require more than a casual technical adjustment, because the longer the shaft of the club, the tougher it is to hit. From out in the fairway, I saw him move to his bag and pull the head cover off a fairway wood. I backed up a few steps guessing the distance that the ball would travel. I watched intently as he started his backswing, slowly moving his club away from the ball. Then, as he swung forward at the ball, all I saw was a blast of turf exploding into the air. The ball jumped forward about 50 yards in front of him. He must have hit inches behind it. Instinctively, I started to take a step toward the ball then realized how silly that would have been.

Mr. Hogan stood looking down at the ground for what seemed like an eternity. Me, I just watched. He leaned on his club with his shoulders slumped and his head hung down toward the ground. It was a picture I'll never forget. For me, it was a confusing feeling. I recall glancing around as though there might be others watching with me. There weren't. It was simply him and me. After a few seconds or so, he walked over to the cart and sat down.

This icon of a man looked suddenly mortal. He was like any other athlete with an injury. He was tired, physically and mentally. I stood there and waited. I knew that Mr. Hogan would eventually stand up and get back to work. I felt helpless knowing there was nothing I could do or offer. There was no cigarette smoke emanating from the cart. He must have simply been asking himself, "Why am I doing this?" It was emotional to me then and still is now.

Finally, Mr. Hogan got up off the cart seat and continued hitting shots. When he was done, I came in and asked him if he was okay. He looked at me and just nodded. I felt empty inside. I wanted to ease his pain, but knew deep down I couldn't. Like any great athlete on a road of recovery, it was all up to him.

THE MOST AMAZING SHOT

I'VE SEEN MANY HOLES-IN-ONE and other amazing shots. I once saw a ball skip off a pond, onto the green and into the hole. Another time I saw a ball ricochet off a tree, onto the green and into the hole for an eagle. Strange things happen in golf. But without question, the most amazing shot I ever saw was one hit by Mr. Hogan in a practice session. It was a shot of no consequence, except that it defied physics.

We had stopped to hit some pitch shots into the eighth hole on Shady Oaks' executive nine. The green is on the crest of a rolling piece of terrain and slopes slightly from back to front. It's a standard green designed to accept shots from straightaway. Mr. Hogan, however, liked to park the cart 40 to 50 yards *behind* the green and hit pitches with the green sloping away from him.

Watching him play these pitch shots was great fun. His shots came in low and hot, struck the down slope with loads of backspin, skipped twice toward the front of the green and stopped dead. It was an incredible thing to see; I never could figure out how he could generate enough clubhead speed, with a swing that short, to impart enough backspin to stop the ball. What's more amazing is he hit most of those shots with a 49-degree pitching wedge!

And that was the case this particular day. His pitches all behaved the same way, except for one. Using a lob-wedge or even a sand wedge would make what I'm about to say understandable ... it's hard to accept the fact that one could do this using a pitching wedge. One of the balls he hit came in low, skipped, halted momentarily, then, to my amazement, climbed back up the slope a good six inches. I stood there for a few seconds, turned to look at him and then stared back down at the ball before I picked it up. I was thinking to myself, "Did I really see that?" If it wasn't a Hogan story, you wouldn't believe me. There was no one else to see it.

As soon as he called me in, I blurted, "Did you know you hit a ball that backed up the slope?" Mr. Hogan shrugged his shoulders and muttered, "Huh?" He didn't understand my comment, and I didn't know how to explain it to him.

I told Nick Faldo this story in 1992 during a flight from Palm Springs, California, to Fort Worth. The next day, Nick grabbed his wedge and we went out to the 8th hole. Nick tried repeatedly to duplicate the shot. He would hit a ball and yell, "Did that one?" We yelled back, "No." He couldn't do it, and I'm willing to bet no one else can, either.

WHAT'S IN A NAME?

EARLY IN OUR EXPERIENCE together, I doubted Mr. Hogan knew my name. One day, a couple of weeks into shagging for him, he sat down in the cart, looked over at me and said, "Hello, Jody. This is a great day, isn't it?" As we had never talked before, I was stunned and only muttered something back to him. After the practice session, we headed back to the shop, where Art Hall was standing outside. After Mr. Hogan disappeared through the shop door, Art walked over to me and said, "Did you hear him call you by name?" I said, "Yeah, is that good?" Art said it must be. He'd never heard Mr. Hogan address anyone who shagged for him by name, with the exception of Old Folks, his tournament caddie.

In retrospect, I think that maybe Mr. Hogan knew it would mean something to me. If so, he was right. I was accepted. It meant the world to me. In the course of a lifetime, having someone acknowledge you is a satisfying feeling. Of course, I would have gone on shagging balls for him for an eternity even if he didn't know my name. Such was the privilege to be a part of those sessions.

3

Disaster in the Pro Shop

BEN HOGAN WAS KNOWN for applying pressure through intimidation. His steely eyes cast a glare that made even the most confident golfers uncomfortable. Holding a half-smoked cigarette and leaning on a club, Mr. Hogan watched you so intensely it was difficult to determine whether he was critiquing your grip or your stance, or was just interested in the shot you were about to play. Only Jack Nicklaus and Tiger Woods have matched Hogan in this area.

One summer morning, I experienced his unnerving glare in the Shady Oaks bag room of all places. It was midweek, and no one else was around. I was 18 at the time, an age where youthful confidence sometimes overtakes common sense. In walked Mr. Hogan carrying a putter in one hand and a rubber putter grip in the other. He asked me where he could find Tom Sisolak, the assistant pro. When I told him he was out running errands, Mr. Hogan looked around anxiously. As I knew Mr. Hogan by now, I took the initiative and asked if I could do something for him.

Mr. Hogan looked at me as if he were sizing me up. Not

a comforting stare. Then he held up the putter and said he wished Tom were around, because he needed a new grip installed. He explained that he didn't want to do it himself because he didn't want to get gas on his hands and have the smell present the whole afternoon as he practiced. (In those days, everybody used gasoline as a solvent to slip grips on golf shafts. The smell lingered forever, though later we'd discovered the trick to eradicating the smell: Washing your hands with everyday toothpaste.)

Casually, I informed Mr. Hogan that Tom had taught me how to replace grips and that I did it all the time. I told him to leave the putter with me, and I would have it finished after lunch when he was ready to go out and practice. Mr. Hogan said that would be fine. But instead of leaving, he said he'd wait and watch me put it on. I don't think he trusted me.

Instantly, I felt a surge of nervousness. I was way beyond my comfort zone. My hands began to sweat. But my pride was at stake, so I decided to get on with it. I took a razor and quickly cut the old grip off the putter shaft. Next, I peeled the old underlying tape off the shaft making it ready for the new grip to be installed. Then, I locked the putter shaft into the vise that was attached to the workbench. So far, so good.

It was at this juncture that Mr. Hogan interrupted the process. He wanted to build up the grip size by wrapping the putter shaft with masking tape before I slipped on the rubber grip. I calmly removed the putter from the vise, handed it to him, and watched as he began wrapping tape around the putter shaft, one layer after another. With each layer, my stress level rose. I thought, "Wow, that's a lot of tape!" Finally, when Mr. Hogan was finished putting on quite a thick buildup of tape, he turned to me and said, "Okay. Put the grip on."

I tried to remain calm, but wasn't feeling all that great. I locked the putter back in the vise. I spread a strip of double-sided adhesive tape over the masking-tape buildup to help lubricate the surface so the grip would slide on more easily. Next, I took the grip and poured some gas down the open end, which would help me get the grip started down the shaft when I slid it on. I lubricated the tape further by spreading a little gas over it. Then, I slid the open end of the grip onto the putter shaft.

That's when the trouble started. The tape was wrapped so thick I had a hard time getting the grip started over the butt of the shaft. After a few hard pushes, the grip started sliding down the shaft like it was supposed to. I felt a momentary sense of relief. But then the grip stopped sliding. Beads of sweat began dripping from my forehead. It was only halfway on. I could hear Mr. Hogan breathing over my shoulder. He hadn't said a word, and I was not about to turn around to elicit any comments from him.

The problem was, the gasoline had evaporated in the hot, dry Texas air, and the adhesive material on the tape had become as sticky as flypaper. What to do? Again, my youthful confidence pushed me forward and told me that this was not a big deal. I took out the trusty old grip remover with the syringe-needle attachment. I inserted the needle through the wall of the grip just above the tape and squeezed the handle, injecting gas under the grip. But as I began pulling the grip off, a section of tape came off along with the grip. A big wad of it hung from the open end. I quickly took a long screwdriver and started fishing out the tape. Mr. Hogan, meanwhile, removed the putter from the vise and started retaping the putter shaft. He didn't say a word, and neither did I. The less I said, the better.

After he finished retaping the shaft, I placed it back in the vise and this time poured enough gas on the tape to burn down the clubhouse. There was not a chance in hell the grip was going to do anything but slide on perfectly. Working fast and furious, I poised the tip of the grip at the butt of the shaft, spread my legs for leverage, and made one big push. Success! The grip was in place!

There was only one problem. The rubber grip had thin walls, and the tiny hole created by the tiny syringe needle had become a huge, inch-long gash squarely in the middle of the grip. I stood there for what seemed like two lifetimes, and then looked up to face the music. Mr. Hogan, who had not uttered a sound to this point, was looking dead at me. There is no way to describe the expression on his face. He grumbled, "I knew there was a chance you would screw it up, so I brought two of 'em. The other one is in my locker. I'll go get it." With that, he turned and trudged off to get the other grip.

As Mr. Hogan was walking out of the golf shop door heading back to his locker, Tom walked in and asked, "What'd Hogan want?" Within a second or two he was laughing so hard I thought he was going to split his sides open.

The second grip went on fine, though I was not there to witness it. Tom did it. Me, I trudged outside with Mr. Hogan's bag in hand and waited at the cart. I don't remember that we talked much more that day. Although, as I recall in the time that followed, he didn't ask me to change another of his grips, which meant I never had to face that legendary Hogan pressure again. For that, I am forever grateful.

4

Tools of the Trade

LOOKING AT OR HOLDING one of Mr. Hogan's clubs was almost a religious experience for some. Everyone from ordinary players to top PGA Tour professionals wanted to hear about his clubs and inspect them if possible, hoping there was some great secret that would help them play better. I was in the bag room at Shady Oaks on countless occasions when a guest would walk in unannounced and ask me where Mr. Hogan's clubs were. We all were trained to explain that Mr. Hogan didn't like anyone handling his clubs. Most people still wanted to at least see them.

Some of the more audacious people would walk straight into the bag room and start looking for his clubs on their own. I enjoyed that part. Even though Mr. Hogan's bag was the only one standing in the room—the rest were stationed horizontally in plywood stalls—it didn't have his name on it. So they never were certain those clubs were his. Fort Worth was Hogan country, you see, and all but a few sets of clubs in the bag room were Hogan models. He played the original

1954 Hogan Personal blade, but there was no way a guest would have known that.

All of the bag room stalkers who were able to identify Mr. Hogan's bag reacted the same way: They got this blank look on their faces and just stood staring at it for a moment. Then, of course, they would reach for a club. My cries of "You can't touch the clubs!" usually didn't deter them. They ignored me and went for the clubs anyway.

One guest refused to put Mr. Hogan's clubs back in the bag. He started pulling all the clubs out as if looking for a secret prize. I had to call in Art Hall, the pro, for backup. We had to practically threaten to have the guy kicked off the property before he would leave the bag room. This was a guest of a member, mind you. That guy had nerve.

Most people didn't mean any harm and just wanted to hold a club to see what it felt like. It was hard to blame them. Sometimes on the weekends or holidays when he wasn't playing, Mr. Hogan would walk into the bag room, go over to his bag and pull out a club. He'd ask me, "Has anybody been fooling with my clubs?" I'd always be honest with him and say yes or no. He never got upset and would just ask us to try to keep the stalkers away. I often wondered how Mr. Hogan knew if someone had touched his clubs. I concluded he might be feeling the oil or perspiration from stalkers' hands on his grips. I knew to always hold them at the bottom of the grip and keep my sweaty hands off the place he gripped the club. Sometimes I'd even put a hand towel around the grip before I held one of them.

Mr. Hogan's set of 14 clubs was comprised as follows: Driver, 3-wood, 4-wood, 2- through 9-irons, pitching wedge, sand wedge and putter. He stopped carrying a 1-iron after it was stolen following the famous shot he hit to the 18th green at Merion in the 1950 Open.

	INDUSTRY STANDARD			HOGAN SPECS			
	LOFT	LIE	LENGTH	LOFT	LIE	LENGTH	SWING WEIGHT
IRONS							
2	19	59	39.25	18	58.5	39	D-1
3	22	60	38.75	21	59	38.5	D-1
4	25.5	60.5	38.25	23	59	38	D-1
5	29	61	37.75	27	59	37.5	D-1
6	32.5	61.5	37.25	31	60.5	37	D-1
7	36	62	36.75	35	60	36.5	D-1
8	40	62.5	36.25	38.5	61	36	D-1
9	44	63	35.75	42	61	35.5	D-1
PW1	46	64	35.5	44	63	35.5	D-1
PW2	52	64	35.5	49	63	35.5	D-1
SW	56	64	35	55	65	35	D-4
WOODS							
DRIVER	9.5	56	45	8	55	43.25	D-2.5
#3	14	55	43	15	55	42.25	D-2.5

FREQUENCY = 269 CYCLES OR 7.2 (PRECISION SCALE)
IRON SHAFTS: APEX 5
GRIPS: FULL CORD/58 ROUND/NAME LABEL TURNED UNDER
AT ADDRESS POSITION THE CLUBFACE WAS FIVE DEGREES OPEN.

I saw Mr. Hogan's clubs often, of course, and hit them. Granted, they were prototype clubs he kept in his bag room locker and not his actual playing set. Some nights, just before I would close up the shop, I would take one of the clubs he was testing over to the third fairway and hit shots with it. It's my understanding that Tiger Woods once hit one of Mr. Hogan's fairway woods. He hit the first one a little sloppy, then he did fine on the next one.

Mr. Hogan's were not remotely similar to anyone else's clubs, pro or amateur. When you set one of his irons down in the address position, your first reaction was that it didn't sit right. All of his irons were very open at address. The heel of the club was ground in such a way that the toe of the club was fanned open about five degrees. To the average player, this is a nightmare view of the clubhead position at address.

Once, after I had known Mr. Hogan for a while, I asked him if he would let me have one of the prototype clubs, a Hogan Special sand wedge. The club wasn't chromed. It was forged out of raw steel and then polished. One day when I knew he wasn't using it any longer, I asked him if I could have it. He looked at me for a few seconds, and I thought he was going to say yes. But then he said no and explained that he didn't want anybody using it because it was a prototype. He told me that he would get me one once they started manufacturing them. And he did. The new ones looked great, but never as good as the one in his stall.

I never asked Mr. Hogan why he had the clubface positioned so open at address. I assumed it was a result of his early days when hooking the ball was a big problem for him. He had a pronounced pronation—or roll of his wrists—away from the ball on the backswing and then again through the hitting area. Strangely, however, he always set the club open at address regardless of whether he wanted to hit a draw or a fade.

The open clubface notwithstanding, his irons had one distinct characteristic. The grips on all his clubs had a reminder—a raised rib built into the bottom side of the grip. It acts as a guide, or reminder, to help the player grip the club the same way every time. Mr. Hogan's club maker, Gene Sheeley, created a reminder in the form of a piece of cord he installed under the grip. It was unusual. To explain, imagine the top of the round grip as 12 o'clock on a clock's face. Most reminders are placed at 6 o'clock. Mr. Hogan liked his rib at 5 o'clock. He preferred rubber cord grips of standard size (or a #58 round by today's code), though the reminder gave one the impression of the grip being wider in diameter. Mr. Hogan had all his reminders set at 5 o'clock to ensure a grip that would place the angle of the clubface in an open position. I remember how Nick Faldo's eyes bulged out when he gripped one of the drivers Mr. Hogan had behind his desk—Faldo was shocked by the face angle at address.

He played a Hogan Apex 5 shaft, which translates into an extra stiff shaft in other brands.

The lofts on Mr. Hogan's irons were slightly stronger than ones of that day. The lofts progressed normally through the set with the exception of the 8-iron, which was 38.5 degrees. I asked Mr. Sheeley why Mr. Hogan wanted the 8-iron to be different, and he said he didn't know.

Another slight variation in his clubs was that all his

lengths were measured from the "playing position." This is a Hogan Company term that describes a position of measuring from the *middle* of the clubface up the shaft to the top ring of the grip. All grips have a ring etched toward the top of a grip just below the grip cap. Most measurements are made from the *heel* of the clubface to the end of the grip. However, Mr. Hogan felt his way was more accurate. Some clubs have long faces and some short ones, which will cause a variation in length if measured from the heel. But using Mr. Hogan's method, the measurements read the same regardless of the length of the face.

A final key factor in how he built his clubs was the hosel angle, which Mr. Hogan called the *under-sling*. This is the angle where the club's hosel meets the bottom of the clubface. Mr. Hogan believed that in designing a club the closer you angled or positioned the shaft toward the center of the clubface, the more control the player had over the clubface and ultimately the ball. That's why Mr. Hogan's clubs had a pronounced under-sling. Looking at his club from the face-front position, there is a distinct bend in the hosel that makes the lie look overly flat, even though, technically, it isn't.

The last two issues he addressed in setting up his clubs focused on the amount of bounce he liked and the clubface's offset. Because of his wrist pronation through impact, Mr. Hogan required little, if any, bounce to his irons. Also, you should keep in mind that in his day, he and his contemporaries played on some really hard and bare fairways.

In some cases, he had negative bounce with the long irons. If you look at the sole of a golf club, you will see a slight roll or curvature that becomes more pronounced with each club. The sole of a 2-iron is basically flat. A 9-iron, on the other hand, has a noticeable roll designed into it. The purpose of bounce is to help the club move through the turf. As a general rule, the amount of bounce matches the number of the club you are holding. For example, a typical 9-iron has nine degrees of bounce.

Some of Mr. Hogan's clubs had negative bounce, which occurs when the leading edge of an iron when placed on a flat surface is lower than the trailing edge of the sole. What this meant is that Mr. Hogan didn't need the club's bounce to help him move the clubhead through the turf. He never dug the ball out of the turf—his divots were very shallow. He merely scraped the turf so that bounce had limited bearing on his ball flight.

His irons had no offset. Offset is a measure of how far behind the shaft the leading edge of the clubface is when looking down at address. If you play with a cavity-backed iron, this is really easy to understand. When you set the club on the ground in your address position and look down at the face, your club has some degree of bend or curve in the hosel. That's offset. Mr. Hogan's irons were not bent in that manner.

Mr. Hogan used personal model irons manufactured in 1954. He never changed sets. Even though he was always testing clubs, the personals were in the bag come tournament time. As much as Mr. Hogan practiced, one would think he would have worn them out, but he didn't. This is because the chrome was thicker and more resilient than it is today.

Mr. Hogan's driver was especially important to him. He believed the driver was the most crucial club in the bag. He saw it as vital not only for distance, but for accuracy. The quality of a drive determines your angle of attack at the pin on your second shot. To that end, he believed in using as stiff a shaft as possible. He believed that, under pressure, a soft shaft will fail you. At 43¼" in length, his driver played to a frequency reading of 269 cycles per minute. That's one strong shaft.

If there's a moral to the story of Mr. Hogan's equipment, it's that you shouldn't try to use clubs like his, but you should follow his lead. Get fitted properly. It's not what's in his bag or any other player's bag that's important, it's what works for you. His success had little to do with the clubs. It had everything to do with understanding how to use them. So, by all means, hit those 10,000 balls he always told you to hit.

5

A Lesson from the Master

LATE ONE AFTERNOON in 1967, after we were done practicing for the day, Mr. Hogan began his customary route back to the clubhouse. He always drove down the right side of the 18th fairway and across the executive nine toward the bridge beside the 18th green. This day, he stopped near the ninth tee box on the executive nine.

Without a word, he got out of the cart, grabbed three balls from his shag bag and took his 8-iron from the bag. I wasn't sure what he was up to. In classic Hogan fashion, he gazed at the pin, took a long drag off his cigarette, tossed it on the ground, looked at the pin again and then addressed the ball.

The pin was about 145 yards away. Mr. Hogan couldn't have known that; he never played by exact yardages. In fact, I had never seen him hit a shot from this location. This whole event was a little different for him. His first shot landed 10 feet from the pin. The next one was close also, and the last one was dead at the flag. They were three terrific shots, and watching Mr. Hogan's body language I could tell he was pleased with the result. It was like he had been working on something, and from these three balls he knew it had worked. Next, out of the blue, he turned to me and said, "You want to know how to hit the ball like that?"

I couldn't say "yes" fast enough. There really was no other possible answer. I might never have this chance again. Mr. Hogan casually walked over to the cart, grabbed three balls from the shag bag, turned around and tossed them on the ground. He said, "Let me see you hit those."

Mr. Hogan had watched me hit balls many times. I often hit balls when the day was slow, in the evenings or before I finished picking up balls from the range. His personal table looked directly out at the practice range, and when I hit balls there I often glanced over and saw him watching me.

But this was too much. I was wearing a pair of tennis shoes, didn't have a glove and my hands were suddenly sweating fiercely. I wasn't warmed up and had just finished shagging two bags of balls. After Mr. Hogan handed me his 8-iron, he walked back to the cart, sat on the corner of the seat and lit another cigarette. Then he told me to hit the shots.

I looked down at that wide-open clubface and felt mortified. I was standing in Fort Worth, and the toe of the club was pointed toward New York when it should have been pointing toward Chicago. It was the most intense pressure I'd ever felt. I quickly hit the three balls, barely stopping to watch them land. Much to my amazement and relief, they all flew right at the flag. They also flew well past the flag, landing on the mounds well over the green. The target was 145 yards away. My shots were flying 160+ yards. It must have been the adrenaline. When I was done, my heart was pounding.

I finally looked over at Mr. Hogan, still perched calmly on the cart. He looked dead at me and said, "That was fine, but they went too far. You can't hit an 8-iron that far and play golf."

I felt taken aback, but not offended by his comment. For all the world, I could have topped the shots, shanked them or, under the circumstances, whiffed them. The last thing I expected was to do what I had done! I thought I'd done a heck of a job. It was like he had expected me to hit the shots I did. It was only later, after I'd gone home, that I realized what a treat that lesson, however short, really was. John Ballard, who was one of the founders of the 7-Eleven Corporation and an old friend of Mr. Hogan's, told me that in all his years he never once saw Mr. Hogan hand over one of his clubs for someone else to hit. That made it even more special.

The day didn't end when I hit my last ball. Mr. Hogan had more to say. It was a lesson of a lifetime from a master of the game. Over the next half hour or so, for whatever reason, Mr. Hogan decided to reveal to me his mysterious "Swing Secret." The one many thought he never told anyone. He told me.

6

The Secret:
A Revelation of Cause and Effect

MANY TIMES OVER THE YEARS, I've reflected on whether Mr. Hogan ever told anyone the same things he told me that summer afternoon in 1967. I've watched, read and listened, expecting to see somewhere the revelation of the Secret he explained to me. After 36 years of waiting, I am convinced he never did.

I thought I might have been wrong when I received the March 1994 issue of *Golf Digest* magazine. On the cover was a drawing of Mr. Hogan at impact and the storyline: "Exclusive: Ben Hogan's Secret." I thought, "Well, maybe this is it." After staring at the cover for a few nervous minutes, I finally opened the magazine and read the article by Guy Yocom. I read very slowly, not wanting to miss a single phrase or thought. Although it's a great article and well worth reading, I realized, much to my surprise, that Mr. Hogan had not shared the swing secret he told to me with anyone quoted in the article.

One fellow came close. Dick Harmon, the son of one of Mr. Hogan's contemporaries, Claude Harmon, quoted his father on Mr. Hogan's strong lateral move on the downswing. It was very close, but I still don't believe his opinion came directly from Mr. Hogan.

Since that day when Mr. Hogan told me his secret, I have struggled over whether to share the secret publicly. While Mr. Hogan was still alive, I dreaded the idea of him discovering that I had betrayed his trust. I had considered asking him about it in 1996 and asked Mrs. Hogan if she thought it was a good idea. She had no objections per se, although she warned me his memory was failing him and he might not remember much of what he told me. I knew that, but I decided not to approach him.

Still, there was evidence Mr. Hogan was willing to share his secret with a wider audience. In 1991, well after he had finished his playing career, he offered to tell his secret to *Golf Digest* for the fee of $100,000, a fee they balked at. Moreover, had Mr. Hogan wanted the secret to die with him, he would never have revealed it to me! I think he told me knowing that some day I would share it with others. And I believe that was ultimately what he wanted. The only issue was timing. With my memoirs of Mr. Hogan now complete, I feel the time is now.

The day he gave me that quick lesson, Mr. Hogan talked about the golf swing for half an hour. He explained to me what he did, and why he did it. He never hit a ball. We simply talked. When I asked a question, he answered it fully and articulately. The Secret he revealed seems simple at first glance, but becomes a bit more complex when you parse out its meaning.

The Secret is the correct functioning of the right leg, with emphasis on maintaining the angle of the right knee on the back and forward swings. Combined with a slight cupping of the left wrist, it produces optimum balance and control, and allows you to apply as much speed and power as you wish.

Not knowing the implications of that simple statement, the first question I asked Mr. Hogan was why I didn't read about his right-knee position being such an important part of his swing in the *Five Lessons* book. He put his hands on his hips and said, "I'm not telling them this!" I could only guess that by "them" he was referring to his fellow competitors. You should recall that Mr. Hogan was still playing competitively at the time he wrote his book.

My next question was about his famous cupped left wrist. Mr. Hogan had explained in a 1955 article for *Life* magazine that his secret was cupping his wrist at the top of the backswing. Hogan was being truthful, but as he revealed to me that day, it was only part of the story. Mr. Hogan explained to me that the left wrist was cupped because it was the only position the wrist could assume based on the position of his right knee.

To cup your wrist, stand erect and extend the left arm forward as though to shake another person's hand. Without bending the arm in the slightest fold the wrist toward the left at a 45-degree angle. Next, twist the shoulders to the right simulating the backswing of a golf motion. Once the arm is past parallel, stop the motion. At this point you can see the back of the left hand. Now you are in a cupped wrist position. So was Mr. Hogan.

To better illustrate all this, Mr. Hogan put me in his address position and then in his position at the top of his backswing. With a twinkle in his eye, he then asked me a simple question: Could I maintain the right-knee position I had at address when I reached the top of the backswing, and feel totally comfortable without cupping my wrist? I couldn't. But, not fully understanding the relationship between the left wrist and the right knee—a cause/effect relationship that would baffle anyone the first time they heard it—I asked him again about the cupped left wrist. He gave me an irritated look and said, "What the hell did I just say about the left wrist?"

Mr. Hogan started over, this time making sure I understood the action of the lower body before explaining the implications of the cupped left wrist. Mr. Hogan explained that he braced his right knee before and after he took the club away from the ball, thus allowing his takeaway to be made with perfect balance. Looking at Mr. Hogan in the address position, it's important to note that his right knee is angled inward (toward the target) markedly. He was giving himself a head start—and a firm point of reference—that would help him maintain this flexed angle. He maintained that right-knee position from address all the way to the top of the backswing. This allowed him to set the club at the top of his backswing and control his transition from backswing to downswing, all the while maintaining his balance. He said the right knee could sway a bit from left to right, but it should *never* straighten, especially as you move to the top of the backswing.

I.

ADDRESS POSITION

2.
TOP OF THE
BACKSWING

3.
CUPPED WRIST AT TOP
OF SWING

Maintaining the flexed-knee position was important to him because he believed that once you lost your knee flex, all of your swing-plane angles drifted out of alignment. Those angles were the clubshaft, shoulders and hips (the same angles he addressed in the *Five Lessons* book). The resulting poor alignments then forced a player to spend the rest of the swing trying to attain the correct angles again, all the while trying to stay in balance.

Thus far, Mr. Hogan has talked only about the backswing. I should add, however, that Mr. Hogan was not focused on his backswing. The downswing was what mattered most. The backswing was merely a preface to the real issue: the delivery of the club back to the ball. His entire goal was to return the club to the ball with balance and control so he could produce the type of ball flight he desired. One issue that is sometimes lost by lesser players is that hitting the ball solidly is paramount. Solid contact, which comes from good balance, evolves into ball control. When Mr. Hogan struck a golf ball, he did so with a distinct type of ball flight in mind. He wanted the ball to go left, right, high, low or some combination therein. To attain that ball flight, he first had to hit the ball on the sweet spot of the clubface.

Now to the cupped left wrist. I suggest you try the following test, as it will demonstrate how it ties in with everything Mr. Hogan has said so far. Take your favorite club in your hands. Now, address the ball. Next, perform the backswing, keeping your right knee flexed as though your entire lower body was still in the position you had at address. To do it, you'll find it necessary to shift most of your body weight onto your right leg. You should feel pressure on three key aspects of your right leg: your ankle, your kneecap and your hip joint. If you feel no pressure, there is too much weight on your left leg. That means a reverse pivot. Mr. Hogan did not reverse pivot.

Also, pay attention to your shoulder turn. At the top, make sure you've turned fully, with your left shoulder occupying a place close to, but not directly over, your right foot. If the knee straightens and loses its flex or the shoulders aren't turned fully, none of the rest of this matters. You may want to move on to the next chapter.

Now, holding that position at the top of your backswing, bow your left wrist outward so the wrist joint is exposed to the sky—the opposite of cupped inward. Do you feel anything? Do you feel you are out of balance? Undoubtedly you are. And this is a bad time to be out of balance in a golf swing.

That's the whole point, the first half of the Secret. If you hold the right knee in a flexed position, and your left wrist is either straight or bowed outward, you will have the sensation you are leaning forward on your toes. You will have the distinct feeling of "coming over the top," even though you still are on your backswing. You have lost your balance. It's over, my friend.

This is why Hogan cupped his left wrist. It kept him in balance. Repeat the exercise I just described, this time cupping your left wrist. You'll immediately feel a sense of stability, balance and control. The more you cup your wrist, the more stable you'll feel. Not that you want to cup your wrist excessively, of course. You want to cup it halfway between being flat and cupped as far as it will go.

The validity of this phenomenon can be proved by going to the opposite extreme. Try cupping the wrist, but allow the right knee to straighten. You've just lost your balance again. You still can't break 80. Make no mistake, the right-knee position *made* Ben Hogan's swing (Hogan said so, I didn't).

But the backswing is only half the story. There is the matter of the downswing, which Mr. Hogan saw as much more crucial. The key to his downswing was that he "Ran his right knee at the ball." What does this mean? On the downswing, Mr. Hogan's first movement was to push the knee inward to the left and toward the ball. This resulted in a lateral shifting and opening of the left hip. His first and only thought had to be the right knee dropping in at the ball. He referred to it that day in an abbreviated fashion: "Running at the ball."

Mr. Hogan explained that the harder he wanted to hit the ball, the faster he ran his right knee at the ball. That's why his hips unwound so fast on the downswing. In his mind, he ran his right knee to the ball, while feeling a complete sense of balance and control. For him, the feeling of his knee was the only thing that mattered—he forgot about everything else in his body during that part of the swing.

When you watch videos of Mr. Hogan's downswing, you can spot how early he shifted his weight to his left side. He did this very aggressively. His hips also unwound much faster than those of an ordinary player. But they are not causes, however. Both movements are made possible by the action of the right knee.

By running the right knee at the ball, Mr. Hogan was able

4.

STARTING DOWN FROM THE BACKSWING

to generate terrific speed in his lower body. His right knee moved so emphatically to the left that on full shots, his right knee would sometimes appear to overtake his left knee on the follow-through. The speed was adjustable, however. By running his knee at the ball at different speeds, he was able to control the amount of force he expended into the ball through impact. This was why he was able to control the ball's distance so precisely.

As the Secret relates to power, Mr. Hogan said in *Five Lessons* that he wished he had "three right hands." He meant he wasn't afraid to apply as much power as he wanted when the situation called for it. But, I feel his meaning was that the right hand to Hogan performed in concert with the actions of his right knee. If he ran his right knee at the ball correctly on the downswing, his right hand could react as desired, and he was free to hit the ball as hard or as softly as he wanted to without the fear of losing control.

When you attempt a swing using the Secret, key the downswing by pushing your right knee inward both to the left and toward the ball. You'll find that your upper body will follow the action of your lower body quite nicely. You should feel distinct pressure on the inside of your right foot, as though you are actually pushing off that foot. The rest should happen automatically, though I've one last note of caution. Make sure you monitor your left knee. You don't want to straighten it too soon; it will cause you to hang back on your right side and the ball can go anywhere. You merely want to straighten your left leg sufficiently for it to absorb

5.
IMPACT POSITION

the transfer of weight from your right side. It should never be locked or rigid at impact.

Remember, the Secret works with every club in the bag. It is especially effective on short irons and longer pitches. Downing Gray, a past Walker Cup captain, relates how the Secret made Hogan such a fine wedge player. Downing was playing a practice round with Mr. Hogan at Augusta. On the seventh hole, the pin was in an impossible front-left position, barely on the green. The other players complained about the hole location, saying it was impossible to play to. Downing said Mr. Hogan heard the complaints, then without a word pulled his wedge from his bag and nipped the ball perfectly, landing it by the hole and stopping it dead in its tracks. The complaining ceased.

Mr. Hogan's last words to me that afternoon were uttered sternly for emphasis. He held out his right index finger next to my face and said: "Don't tell anybody I told you this." When we got back to the golf shop I put up his clubs and walked out to the front counter where Tom was closing out the daily records. I leaned on the glass counter, thought for a minute and then walked back into the bag room. So I kept the Secret a secret for 25 years, revealing it to no one except Nick Faldo (I rationalized I had to tell someone who would understand it). To reveal a secret to only one person over the course of 36 years is a reasonable display of confidence, I suppose. I think Mr. Hogan would be fine with that.

Good luck with it and now, go hit your 10,000 balls!

7

The Trials of a Teacher

CHILDREN COMMONLY INHERIT the physical features of their parents. Quite often they display the same mannerisms as well. As Mr. Hogan had such a profound influence on me as a golfer, friends have wondered aloud why my own swing bears no resemblance at all to Mr. Hogan's. Although I became a scratch player and enjoyed moderate success in amateur competition, the swing I formulated is my own. The reason is simple: From the moment I began working for Mr. Hogan, I knew instinctively that I could never swing the club like him.

Outstanding golfers are often so full of talent and natural ability that they make the most difficult swing movements look easy. They may be exciting to watch, but trying to imitate them can be intimidating and foolhardy. In the case of Mr. Hogan, he spoke to me at length about the golf swing, but the adage that the best players don't necessarily make the best teachers held true. He could explain swing mechanics articulately, but couldn't always communicate that innate feel and instinct that made him a great player.

For years I saw Mr. Hogan hit shots that I tried to copy but couldn't. I saw him hit amazing shots that I decided right away I could never hit. I also knew that he hated to give lessons, which made me hesitant to approach him for advice about some aspect of the swing I was working on. Mr. Hogan did give lessons early in life when he held a club job, but he never liked teaching per se. It was only after he quit playing competitively that he became willing to watch a few players.

His tactic when asked a golf-related question was to hand out advice in short comments or quick thoughts. He wasn't trying to be rude. It was his nature. He never wanted to go to the driving range with a player to explain it. Much of his reluctance had to do with his unwavering belief that players had to practice by themselves to figure out their own swing. That's how he did it. To him, there was no other way.

The truth is: You didn't want a lesson from Ben Hogan. You might never recover! He was impatient, and some of the things he asked of his pupils were darned near impossible. Unlike teachers today, he focused all his comments and instruction on what worked for him. He lacked the mental flexibility and imagination necessary to help a student adopt a swing based on their innate tendencies and instincts. That's why when Mr. Hogan did make an exception to his no-lesson rule, the results were not always in favor of the person on the receiving end.

I only saw him give a couple of lessons the whole time I was at Shady Oaks. And, while the lessons were rare, they were also unforgettable in the way that Mr. Hogan could make any encounter unforgettable.

The Agonies of R. K. Hanger

For some mysterious reason, Mr. Hogan always took great pains to help R. K. Hanger, a lawyer whose firm handled some of Mr. Hogan's personal affairs. I always wondered why. Hanger had no chance at ever hitting a shot that anyone would ever want to hit. From tee to green, he was just dreadful. A super nice gentleman, but couldn't play a lick.

All of the guys in the golf shop used to call Hanger "The Black Knight." He was in his mid 60s, stood about 5-foot-5 and weighed more than 200 pounds. He had a short, squatty body and was rather bowlegged. His was not an athletic figure. His hair was pure white, and his skin had a pinkish hue. His slacks or shirt—and sometimes both—were jet black. Mr. Marvin had a policy of letting certain members own their golf carts and keep them in the club's cart barn. Hanger's was an old ClubCar model with a rounded front that was jet black with a white seat. To me it looked like a chariot. Hence, The Black Knight.

Mr. Hogan loved to give R. K. Hanger lessons, and they were a wonder to witness. Hanger would walk into the shop and ask for his cart and clubs. He never played or practiced during the week, so when he came in, I knew why he was there.

"Are you going to play a few holes, Mr. Hanger?" we'd ask him. He would inevitably reply: "No, I have to take a goddamn lesson from Hogan!" We'd look at him and laugh or smile. He genuinely was irritated. A few minutes later Mr.

Hogan would appear and off to the range the two would go, in separate carts, no less.

Tom Sisolak and I would watch from the golf shop window and marvel at the spectacle that then took place.

One of the drills Mr. Hogan had Hanger perform was something to behold. It was a drill that I had seen teachers use before, though personally I never understood its point. Mr. Hogan would have Hanger lift his club straight out in front of him, where it was parallel to the ground. In the second motion, he cocked his wrists, creating a 90-degree angle between his arms and the club, which was now pointed at the sky. Then Hanger would turn his big shoulders as far as he could, thus simulating a full backswing position. Finally, Hanger would try to hit the ball.

Without fail, Mr. Hanger either missed the ball completely, shanked it or hit a grounder back to the pitcher's mound. Never once did he ever hit a good shot. Mr. Hogan would watch and continue giving instruction. After about 15 minutes, Mr. Hogan would jump back in his cart and head back to the clubhouse. As he walked past us, he would always make some positive comment like, "I think he's got it now." Hanger, to his credit, would stay on the driving range doing this drill until his pile of practice balls was gone.

Every time, when Hanger was finished, he'd walk back through the shop, grumbling to himself and probably thinking about how many aspirins he'd need to calm the soreness he'd experience later. I never asked Hanger what he had learned, and he never said anything to me. Often I've found that golfers will finish a lesson and want to talk endlessly about how much they've learned from it. Hanger never did.

That was Hanger's "Hogan moment." He had more than his fair share.

Big moment for "Tiny" Gooch

One of R. K. Hanger's law partners was a fellow named J. A. "Tiny" Gooch. A former football player at the University of Texas, Tiny stood about 6-foot-5 and was very big all around. In his 60s at the time, he was a 12-handicapper with a short, quick swing that frequently produced terrible hooks.

Mr. Hogan and I were driving back to the golf shop after a day of practice. As we drove by the driving range, Tiny started waving at us to stop. Mr. Hogan was looking the other way and didn't stop. I noticed that Mr. Gooch scrambled over to his cart and followed us down to the golf shop. As Mr. Hogan was signing my caddie ticket, Tiny walked up and placed his hand on Mr. Hogan's shoulder. Mr. Hogan turned when he felt Tiny's hand on his shoulder and looked up at Tiny towering above him. Tiny said flatly, "Ben, I need a lesson. I have a horrible hook and I can't stop it." Mr. Hogan put his hand on Gooch's shoulder and said, "Tiny, go back up there, hit 10,000 balls and then come talk to me. I promise if you'll hit 10,000 balls, you will get rid of that hook or at least know how to play it."

Ten thousand balls! It was easily one of Mr. Hogan's

favorite sayings. Truly he did believe that you were your own best teacher. If you spent the time to dig the answer out of the ground as he had done, you would be better for it.

That didn't satisfy Tiny. He said, "I understand, Ben, but right now, today, I can't get my driver off the ground. It hooks so fast I can't even get it in the air."

Mr. Hogan looked over at me and then at Tiny again. "Jody, go get Tiny's driver," he said, and I retrieved Tiny's big, black Hogan-model persimmon driver—his favorite club. What happened next was something to see. Without a word, Mr. Hogan walked straight over to the workbench and clamped the shaft of the driver into a vise. "You sure you hook this driver?" he asked.

"Yes, but, Ben, that's my favorite club," said Tiny, both confused and sensing the worst.

Mr. Hogan nodded, braced his legs, arched his back, grabbed the driver head with both hands and pulled the driver head toward him. The driver started bending right at the neck where the nylon whipping secures the hosel to the shaft. The club made some strange noises and looked as if it were about to snap in two pieces.

Finished twisting and pulling, Mr. Hogan calmly unlocked the vise, set the club on the floor and looked carefully at the club. Finally, he handed the club to Gooch. When Tiny set the club down in the address position, he looked on the verge of having a heart attack. The face was now open to the right by a whopping 10 degrees—impossible to hook, but also impossible for a mere mortal to use effectively. Mr. Hogan reached over, patted Gooch on the left arm and said, "Tiny, you'll never hook that club again." Then he walked out of the bag room and straight for the locker room.

Tiny Gooch never asked Mr. Hogan for help with his game again.

TOM SISOLAK

TOM SISOLAK, the first assistant at Shady Oaks, was a superb ball striker. A couple of years after I left the club, some members financed Tom on the PGA Tour. If Tom could have putted a lick, he'd still be out there. He was a first-rate player.

One afternoon after Mr. Hogan had hit balls, we were driving by the practice tee and saw Tom there, pounding drivers. Mr. Hogan drove the cart up on the tee and stopped beside Tom's pile of balls. Hellos were exchanged. We watched for a couple of minutes as Tom belted out one 300-yard drive after another, every one displaying just the hint of a draw.

Mr. Hogan got out of the cart, walked over to Tom and began explaining to him that his hips were not quite right. Mr. Hogan explained that Tom's hips should be more open at impact with his belt buckle facing the target as the club struck the ball. This was something Hogan thought he did with his own swing, but did not. His hips were open, but not to the extent he believed. Sometimes things a player feels occur in the swing are different from what actually does occur. Even for a player of Mr. Hogan's caliber.

Tom listened to Mr. Hogan intently. Then fully understanding his Hogan instruction, he teed up another ball and let it fly. The ball rocketed straight right at a 45-degree angle, dead into the middle of the 10th fairway, which is to the right of the driving range. This was close to 50 or 60 yards offline, a solid, but horrible shot. Tom looked over at Mr. Hogan expectantly and I think somewhat embarrassed. Mr. Hogan nodded his head in approval and told him to keep working on that. Then we drove off to the golf shop.

Mr. Hogan thought he'd put Tom on the right track, and in truth the tip might have worked for Mr. Hogan. But somehow I have the feeling that Tom never used that tip again.

HIGH HOPES FOR JAY HEBERT

IN 1968, MR. HOGAN GOT A CALL from Gardner Dickinson, whom he'd played and worked with during their days on tour. It was the week of the Colonial PGA Tour Tournament and Gardner wanted to know if he and Jay Hebert, a fine player and winner of the PGA Championship in 1960, could come over to Shady Oaks for his "Hogan moment," which would be a swing lesson from Mr. Hogan. Hebert, Gardner explained, was in a terrible slump. Perhaps Hogan could help him.

Mr. Hogan agreed, which to me was something of a surprise. Very rarely did he give in to requests such as this. It must have had something to do with the genuine friendship that existed between Gardner and Mr. Hogan. In any event, Gardner and Hebert arrived and I accompanied the three men to Mr. Hogan's private practice area by the No. 11 green.

The lesson dragged on for hours. It bordered on being

brutal. Mr. Hogan kept working and working on Hebert's leg action. He was hitting the ball terribly with lots of snap-hooks and blocked shots to the right. Poor Hebert didn't have a clue where the ball was going. Every now and then, Mr. Hogan got frustrated and told Gardner to grab a club and demonstrate what he was trying to tell Hebert. Dickinson could do exactly what Mr. Hogan wanted, but Hebert could not.

Finally, almost two hours into the lesson, Mr. Hogan said, "Jody, get my balls and head out there." I grabbed the shag bag, dumped his balls on the grass and ran to where Gardner's caddie had been standing, about 275 yards out. When Gardner's caddie saw me running toward him, he figured his day was done. He was exhausted. He'd been running all over the place chasing Hebert's drives. He sat down and stretched out on a towel spread on the ground.

I set the shag bag on the ground a few yards in front of me and waited for Mr. Hogan to begin hitting. Without a warm-up, he let his first shot fly. The ball hit the ground, bounced and jumped directly into the shag bag, which I had placed in front of me.

This was not a big deal to me or anyone else that had ever shagged balls for Mr. Hogan. If he was hitting a 7-iron or less, balls often went into the bag. The first time it happened, you'd think, "Wow! Bet he can't do that again." But you soon realized that balls hopped into the shag bag all the time. It was a game to me; I used to guess which club he would use to land a ball in the bag next. It was a great way to kill time (shagging balls can be a boring job).

I hesitated before retrieving the ball from the bag. It occurred to me that maybe this caddie, whom I did not know, had never seen a player hit a shot that went into the bag. Especially one hit with a driver. I turned around to see if he had anything to say. He didn't miss a beat. He looked at me and said, "Man, you ain't got no job." We both laughed. It was only years later, upon reminiscing with Hebert about the day, that he informed me the caddie was none other than Herman Mitchell, who worked for Lee Trevino for many years.

Eventually the lesson ended and we started back to the clubhouse. About halfway in, Mr. Hogan looked over at me and said, "That son of a bitch better play good tomorrow, with all the work we put into him." The following day, Thursday, the first day of Colonial, Mr. Hogan walked through the shop and asked me, "What did he shoot?" I told him: "Red Grange ... 77." Mr. Hogan didn't say a word to me directly, but he muttered something unintelligible to no one in particular.

Many years later, during the Champion's Dinner held on the eve of the Colonial Tournament, I was standing at the head table talking with Mr. Hogan. I told him the Hebert story, which he had totally forgotten about. But, when I told him Herman Mitchell's punch line from that day, it was the hardest I ever saw Mr. Hogan laugh.

8

Adventures in Putting

WHEN YOU THINK OF Ben Hogan, you don't think of putting. At least not in a positive way. While the Hogan name was synonymous with superior ball striking, it also brought to mind the depths of putting misery. As has been the case with many great champions, Mr. Hogan was an excellent putter in his prime. But at the end of his career, he, like so many others, faltered with the short stick.

Somebody once asked him what his dream course would look like if he ever had the chance to build it. He described it as having greens with a three-foot concave circular slope around every cup. If you were good enough to hit your approach shot that close to the pin, you were rewarded. The ball would go in the hole and you didn't have to putt at all. He immediately laughed, but I think he meant it.

THE MAN WHO LOATHED PRACTICE

MR. HOGAN HATED PUTTING so much that he didn't even want to talk about it. As I cautioned many people through the years, if you wished to end a meeting with Mr. Hogan, start talking about putting. Still he always worked to improve at it at the time I was around him, near the end of his career. Even though he was no longer a threat to win, he still practiced putting as hard as you'd expect any professional golfer to. But I feel he had to force himself to practice putting.

As with his other practice routines, the ever-private Mr. Hogan found a place to practice his putting away from everyone else. Henry Martin, the Shady Oaks course superintendent in the 1960s, would cut two putting holes about 15 feet apart on the back of the second green for Mr. Hogan to use. His full-swing practice complete, he would drive back to the golf shop, park his cart and pull out his putter and three balls. For the next 30 minutes or so, he worked on his putting.

Mr. Hogan rarely asked me to go over to the putting green with him, and never over to the second hole. When Mr. Hogan wanted me to stay with him, he would say so. We would go over to the main putting green, where he practiced both chipping and putting. It was standard caddie work: I'd walk around retrieving his shots and tossing them back to him.

When he practiced short putts, I'd sit behind the hole and toss the balls back. By my calculations, I've watched Mr. Hogan hit thousands of putts. I must admit, he didn't make a very high percentage at that stage in his life. When he putted from 10 to 15 feet, he usually made about two of six. Many times he didn't make any. I can remember thinking to myself, "I can putt better than this guy." One day I got my chance to prove it.

A TRICK MR. HOGAN NEVER LEARNED

ON A SLOW DAY, I killed time by hitting putts from the pro shop sales counter to the doorway of the bag room. It's a distance of about 15 feet. From this location, I could watch for the members coming up from the parking lot and also be close enough to answer the phone behind the counter.

I used a practice putting cup, the type that has several metal strips attached in a circle around the center. When you putted, the ball would roll over the strips, which would tilt inward dropping the ball in the center as if the ball had gone in a cup. It worked great.

One day Mr. Hogan walked in while I was putting. We exchanged hellos and he leaned on the counter and watched me hit a few putts. Now, I had been putting from this spot for a long time. Over time I had learned exactly where to hit the putt. If you hit a spot about three feet from the ball's starting point, the ball would settle into a carpet groove and go straight in the cup. Once I hit the spot, the rest was a matter of speed. If you got the ball to the carpet groove, it went in every time.

Of course, Mr. Hogan didn't know that. He watched me

make putt after putt until he couldn't stand it anymore. He asked for the putter and hit a couple of putts. Each ball missed the center of the cup and rolled off the carpet onto the concrete floor in the bag room. I retrieved the balls and tossed them back to him. He putted a few more with the same results. He continued to putt and made a couple but missed most of them.

Finally he stopped, handed me back my putter and again leaned against the counter. I started putting again. I knocked my first ball into the cup. Since the cup was only big enough to hold one ball at a time, I walked over to retrieve the ball so I could hit the next one. As I walked toward the cup, I noticed Mr. Hogan was leaving. As I turned, he said, "I could make 'em too if I cut the ball with my putter."

Obviously, Mr. Hogan didn't approve of my taking the clubhead outside on the backswing and then making the putt anyway. With that he walked out the door. I never told him that the stroke didn't matter. All you had to do was hit the carpet groove to make the ball go in every time. Besides, he probably thought then, like we do today, that kids often make everything they look at because it hasn't yet dawned on them how difficult putting really is.

I wasn't quick enough to say anything in response and Mr. Hogan was out the door before I realized it. Plus I figured Mr. Hogan didn't care to listen to some kid tell him how to putt on a carpet—I knew even then that he wasn't particularly fond of talking about putting in general.

ONE MAGICAL DAY

MR. HOGAN WAS PRACTICING 10-foot putts on the putting green one day, which was a common exercise for him. I was sitting behind the hole as usual. What was not common was that all of a sudden he started making everything. He was putting with six balls, and for whatever reason he made all six in a row. I tossed the balls back to him, and he made six more. At this point, I didn't look up at him because I didn't quite know how to react. He had never gotten this hot with the putter before.

Then he made the next six—that's 18 in a row! I tossed the balls back. Not a word was said. By now, I knew he knew that I knew this was not normal. He addressed the next putt and made it. After I watched it go in the hole, I finally couldn't resist taking a peek. I looked straight up at him.

Mr. Hogan was already addressing the next ball, but he could either feel me looking at him or else saw my head motion out of the corner of his eye. While still looking down at the ball, he paused for a split second and started to grin. Then he glanced at me for just a brief second and then back to the ball. When our eyes met, it was a "can-you-believe-what-you-just-saw" look. Nothing was said.

He hit the next putt and missed. Then he putted the other four balls—they all missed. His last batch of six balls gone, he turned, walked back to his bag, dropped the putter in and headed to the pro shop. I followed him into the shop, where he signed my caddie ticket. We never said a word to each other.

It was a crazy few minutes in time that I shared with him. Even though it appeared Mr. Hogan was doing something that was totally meaningless, at that moment I knew it was as rewarding to him as anything he could have been doing. He enjoyed having success on the golf course—whether it was winning a major or making 19 putts in a row in practice.

LAGGING FOR DOLLARS

THERE WAS A FELLOW with the Hogan Company back in the '60s named Jack Blades. He was the plant's general manager sent to Fort Worth to run the operation after AMF Inc. bought the brand.

One day after Mr. Hogan and I had just finished practicing and he had gone to the back of the second green to putt by himself, Blades and another gentleman walked into the golf shop. They were both in business suits with cocktails in hand. They watched Mr. Hogan putt for a minute from inside the shop, and then the man with Blades said, "Too bad he can't putt anymore." Blades smiled and said, "He's a good putter on long putts."

I could see where this was going. The guy said, "No way." So Blades said that he'd bet him $100 that Mr. Hogan could get two out of three putts from where Hogan was standing to within three feet of the pin on the front of the second green. The distance was 50 to 60 feet. The guy jumped at the bet and out the door they went. I wanted to go too—$100 was a lot of money in 1965. But I thought better of it and watched from the door.

They walked over to Mr. Hogan. Blades introduced the guy and they shook hands. Then Blades pointed over to the pin toward the front of the green. Mr. Hogan said something I couldn't hear, and they all laughed. Next, Mr. Hogan pulled a ball over, addressed it and hit the first putt. The ball stopped close to the hole. He hit the next one. By the time the ball stopped, Blades was grinning from ear to ear. He slapped his friend on the back, and the pigeon promptly reached into his pocket, took a bill from his money clip and handed the $100 to Blades.

Then Blades trotted down to the pin, picked up the balls and brought them back to Mr. Hogan. After they shook hands, Blades and his friend came back through the shop heading back to the 19th hole. Mr. Hogan, quite satisfied, I'm sure, returned to his putting practice as if nothing had happened.

A DEADLY CHIPPER

So you can see that while short putts were murder for Mr. Hogan—as everyone in the golfing world knew—long putts were not a problem for him. This could be partially explained if you think of effective putting in terms of distance rather than direction. In that case, the fact that Mr. Hogan was an accomplished long putter made sense. That's because Mr.

Hogan always was—and still was at that point in his career—a great chipper of the ball.

During our practice sessions, I watched him chip ball after ball into the cup. The distance was irrelevant and so was the club he was using. From the edge of the green, he could use a wedge or a 7-iron and in both cases many of his shots went in. He had an uncanny instinct for how far to hit the ball.

Mr. Hogan's approach to chipping the ball was strictly old school. His clubface opened on the backswing and closed on the follow-through. That meant he always hit the ball on the bottom portion of the clubface. Modern teachers promote a square-to-square clubface because it's an easier shot to make and it's a more consistent shot for those golfers who don't practice a lot. But, when you do this, the ball has a way of climbing up the clubface and feeling less solid.

After watching Mr. Hogan's clubface fan open and then shut after ball impact, I started trying it. I've learned that this swing produces much better shots even if you only slightly open and roll the clubface. The contact is extremely solid and the ball rolls as perfectly as if you'd tossed it with your hand.

This superior chipping stroke once inspired Mr. Hogan to adapt it to his putting stroke! I know. I couldn't believe it either. I was sitting behind the hole as usual and he's making a reasonable number of chip shots from 20 feet or so. All of a sudden he tells me to go get his putter. I jump up, grab the putter out of his bag and hand it to him. He walks onto the putting surface, addresses a ball and makes a chipping-type stroke at the ball. At first the stroke had a weird effect on the ball. The ball bounced, jumped and generally looked horrible. Then he started to hit the ball with some consistency, and it started to roll okay. Still, despite a more consistent stroke, none of the putts went in. This lasted about 15 minutes until he finally stopped, looked over at me and held out the putter. That was the end of that. But it demonstrated once again that Mr. Hogan was always thinking and always willing to experiment with anything that would improve his putting.

THE NON-TRADITIONALIST

IT MAY SOUND HARD to believe, but Ben Hogan, the arch-conservative traditionalist, tried the long putter. Yes, you heard me correctly! He walked into the shop one day carrying a putter with a driver shaft in it. The grip was in the middle of the shaft at the height you would normally find it on a putter, and the shaft extended above the grip. He stuck it in his bag and off we went to hit balls. I had never seen anything like it; the long putter didn't exist in the 1960s. After the usual practice session we headed to the putting green.

Mr. Hogan placed the long part of his shaft under his left arm and anchored it under his armpit. I don't think it occurred to him to place the shaft against his chest, the way it's done today. Looking back, I wish I had thought to ask Gene Sheeley, Hogan's club builder, what he thought when Hogan asked him to make the long putter.

The long putter didn't even make it through one putting

session. Mr. Hogan did leave it in his bag stall, and I saw him pull it out to look at from time to time. But he never took it to the green again. I tried it a couple of times, but knowing what I know today, it did raise some unanswered issues. Still, I knew he must have thought the long putter had possibilities. Mr. Hogan had a habit of keeping the clubs he wasn't finished experimenting with in his bag room stall.

My Hogan Putter

ONE OF MY MOST PRIZED POSSESSIONS is a putter Mr. Hogan gave me. Ironically, it's a Titleist putter. Even the old Hogan staff guys will tell you that the Hogan Company did not make good putters. I thought they were terrible. I putted once with Mr. Hogan's copper blade putter, an Exact Balance model with a center-shaft design. It felt horrible. I assumed that the same model Mr. Hogan used was different—a special alloy, maybe—but it wasn't.

Engraved on the back of the putter he gave me are the words: 1967—AMERICAN RYDER CUP TEAM—BEN HOGAN— CAPTAIN. It's a flanged bulls-eye model. The company gave one to each of the Ryder Cup team members and the team captain, Ben Hogan. Someone told me they were the first 13 made of the model. Titleist also gave each player a mallet-style putter with the same engraving.

In 1967, Mr. Hogan was Ryder Cup captain for the matches played in Houston at Champions Golf Club. That was the year he addressed the crowd and made the famous statement that the United States was going to win because on his side of the table were the 12 best players in the world. He was right, but the statement seemed out of character for him. He wasn't cocky or conceited. He was genuinely a shy man, and open praise seemed to make him uncomfortable. Many times I saw people lavish praise upon him. He would look to the side and down, shake his head, smile and then politely walk away.

After the Ryder Cup, he put the two Titleist putters in his stall. I was able to try both designs late in the day when it was safe to do so and decided I liked the blade better. I knew he would never use either one in competition, because they didn't have "Hogan" stamped on them. Many a night I would take the blade design out and putt with it. I loved it. Titleist hadn't released that model yet, so I was dying to get one. In the shop after practice one day, Mr. Hogan grabbed a caddie ticket and was about to sign for my caddie fee. I stopped him and said, "Mr. Hogan, instead of paying me today, would it be all right if I asked you to give me one of your clubs?" When he asked me which one I wanted, I invited him to follow me back to his bag stall so I could show him. I was nervous about asking, but obviously not so nervous that I didn't ask at all. I leaned over and pulled out the Titleist blade putter.

Mr. Hogan took the putter from me and looked at it for a few seconds, which seemed like an eternity to me. Finally, he said, "Okay." Then he walked back to the shop counter and signed my caddie ticket to pay me for the afternoon anyway. I tried to stop him from signing the ticket, but he just looked over at me, signed it and headed to the locker room.

That the putter had historical significance meant nothing to me at the time. I was just a young, naïve golfer. I liked the putter and I wanted to use it. I putted with it for months and treated it like any other club in my bag. I even put a strip of lead tape on the back of the putter. I wanted to cover his name and the engraving because I was tired of explaining to people where I got the Ben Hogan Titleist putter.

Some years later, Paul Darwin, who succeeded me as the person who shagged balls for Mr. Hogan, saw the putter in my extra club rack and asked if he could use it. I had switched to another putter by then, so I loaned it to him and then forgot about it. Literally. Eight or nine years later, Paul called me at home and said he'd found an old putter that I had loaned him a long while ago. He wanted to know if I'd like it back. He mentioned that the putter was the one with Mr. Hogan's name on it. I accepted the putter, and you can bet it is in a safe place now.

YOU CAN'T HIT WHAT YOU CAN'T SEE

THERE ARE ATHLETES, and then there are athletes. I'm old school. You put on the uniform and play. If you need a time-out, you take it. You don't make excuses that your migraine headache ruined your day. Mr. Hogan was old school.

Everyone wondered how Mr. Hogan had become such a bad short-range putter. Most people wrote it off to the yips, which besets many golfers, as they get older. But there is another side to it, a side few people outside Mr. Hogan's inner circle were aware of.

In 1994, I had a long conversation with Mrs. Hogan that wandered into many areas. One of the topics was Mr. Hogan's putting. She acknowledged that Mr. Hogan's short putting gave him fits, and for the first time revealed why: He couldn't see clearly out of his left eye. In all the time I shagged balls for Mr. Hogan, watching him hit thousands of putts, he never talked about it. I doubt anyone other than the Hogans and perhaps their doctor knew the extent of his vision problems.

In the 1949 Greyhound bus accident, he almost lost the eyesight in his left eye. It was not widely reported because his other injuries were of a life-threatening nature. After he had recuperated, he never talked about the eye injury. Especially how the vision in his left eye deteriorated badly as time passed.

The blurred vision was similar to placing a piece of transparent Scotch tape over your left eye. You can see, but not very well. It had little effect on putts of 15 feet or longer because on that length of putt it's okay to move your head and follow the ball down the intended line. He didn't make many of those, but who does? Short putts were another matter entirely. Part of the problem was physical—he simply couldn't discern the correct line very well. But it also became psychological. You can't trust what you can't see, and the seeds of doubt eroded his confidence. Add to that the pressure of needing to make short putts to be competitive, and you have a recipe for disaster.

As Mrs. Hogan told me this story, I could see the pain in her eyes. She said she reflexively wanted to tell the people in the gallery that Mr. Hogan couldn't see well, but he wouldn't allow it. Her most vivid memory, she said, was at Baltusrol Golf Club during the 1967 U.S. Open—the last one Mr. Hogan played in. On the greens he stood over the ball forever. When she saw him flinch after missing a short putt, she knew it was not from the yips but from sheer frustration. Mrs. Hogan remembered going back to the hotel room and sitting on their bed crying. She pleaded with her husband to tell the press that he couldn't see out of his left eye. But, ever stubborn and ever private, he told her that he would not say a word and forbid her from saying anything as well. There would be no excuses for his play. Can you imagine today's player keeping that a secret?

As comical as it may seem, Mrs. Hogan's revelation answered a question that to me was personal and stayed with me for years. When Mr. Hogan drove across the bridge on the 18th hole to the clubhouse after practicing, he always drove close to the right side of the bridge railing. There were tree limbs hanging over that side and I always had to lean toward Mr. Hogan to avoid being scratched by those tree limbs as we drove across. It always struck me as curious that he couldn't drive closer to the left side and avoid the branches! When Mrs. Hogan told me about his eye problem, I had my answer.

9

A Visitor Calls

A SHORT PSYCHOLOGICAL PROFILE of a dominant player's traits might read: driven to excellence, focused on winning, relentlessly hardworking, bent on improving, intensely competitive, intimidating and aloof to opponents, analytical, consumed by detail and equally dependent on skill and power. Ben Hogan? It could be, or is it yet another player cut from a similar cloth?

In the fall of 1992, I received a phone call from Harold Riley, an exceptional British artist and friend of mine. Over dinner at the Spanish Open, Nick Faldo mentioned to Harold his long-standing desire to meet Ben Hogan. Harold relayed the request to me, knowing of my Hogan relationship, and asked if I could help. I went to work setting things in motion with what turned out to be an interesting set of circumstances. First I phoned Mr. Hogan's secretary, Doxie Williams, and asked if Mr. Hogan could set aside some time the following week to meet with Nick and his agent, John Simpson. Doxie discussed the idea with Mr. Hogan, who agreed to the meeting with one stipulation: I was not to tell anyone that the meeting was going to take place. Mr. Hogan was concerned that other PGA Tour players would also request a visit, and he wanted to avoid that. I don't think that Mr. Hogan would have minded meeting with other players; it's just that they didn't have a convenient way of accessing him and thus he didn't embrace the notion of fielding calls at random.

The meeting was set for the following Friday morning at 10:30. A problem developed soon after. Nick explained he had to attend a photo shoot late Thursday evening, which made it impossible for him to catch a commercial flight from Palm Springs to Fort Worth that evening. Nick suggested we change the meeting to Saturday morning at Mr. Hogan's home rather than his office. I replied that this was out of the question. Mr. Hogan never had weekend meetings, and visiting him at his house was impossible. I told Nick I could ask the question, but the likelihood was the meeting would be canceled altogether. To Nick's credit, he moved on.

There was one solution: a chartered flight. I arranged for a jet to fly from Fort Worth to Palm Springs, pick up Nick and John and return to Fort Worth. The cost would be $8,800, a considerable sum in the days before players flew private planes routinely. Nick didn't hesitate at the cost, so on Thursday I boarded the plane to Palm Springs and we picked up Nick and Simpson. By 10:30 P.M. we were at my house eating Railhead BBQ.

On the plane I debriefed Nick on what to expect. I suggested that he not get lost in the thrill of meeting Mr. Hogan, because the clock would be running. I suggested that he come prepared, with a written list of specific topics. Silence was deadly with Hogan and you didn't want a lull in the conversation. I told him the meeting would run about 30 minutes at most. I explained how he would know when the meeting was coming to a close; Mr. Hogan would start politely looking at his watch.

There was one final directive: He must not, under any circumstances, discuss putting. Not unless he wanted to end the meeting prematurely.

We had breakfast at Colonial the following morning and headed over to the Hogan plant. There was a short delay in getting there; Nick, in near panic, had forgotten his copy of *Five Lessons* he was dying to have Mr. Hogan sign for him, and we had to hurry back to my house to retrieve it. We arrived at the receptionist's desk at 10:30 A.M. sharp. Doxie came into the lobby to greet us and take us back to his office.

Mr. Hogan greeted us while standing beside his oversized wooden desk. We moved to our seats. I sat to Mr. Hogan's right, David Hueber, the outgoing president of the Hogan Company, sat to the left, and Nick and John sat directly across from Mr. Hogan. We exchanged pleasantries for a few minutes and then Nick got down to business.

Nick Faldo is a great student of the game and a voracious learner. With great purpose, he folded his arms and leaned forward with his elbows on Mr. Hogan's huge desk. He looked across at Mr. Hogan and asked, "How do you win the U.S. Open?"

Mr. Hogan paused, blinked a couple of times and with

his arms resting on his chair's armrest leaned forward looking directly at Nick and said, *"You shoot the lowest score."*

There was a couple of seconds of silence, and then we all burst out laughing. Everyone, except Mr. Hogan. Nick looked over to me and in semi-shock looked back at Mr. Hogan and said, "No, seriously." Mr. Hogan, glancing over toward me, said, "Seriously, I'm not kidding. If by Sunday evening you have shot the lowest score, I promise they will give you the medal. I know. I have *five* of them." The laughter had stopped. Mr. Hogan, in character, was being serious. We immediately understood.

Note that Mr. Hogan said he had five U.S. Open medals, not four as he is credited in the record books. In 1942, the U.S. Golf Association did not hold its official Open due to World War II. Instead the USGA co-sponsored the Hale America National Open in Chicago with many of the trappings of a U.S. Open, including giving a medal to the winner. Mr. Hogan received the medal when he won the championship, but it was never recognized as an official U.S. Open (I wish they would get over it, but it's the USGA, so nobody is surprised).

A number of questions followed, all of which Hogan answered. Nick then set his *Five Lessons* book in front of Mr. Hogan and asked if he would sign it. Mr. Hogan flipped through a couple of pages, scanning it as though he had never seen the book. Nick reached over the desk, pointed to a page bearing the Anthony Ravielli sketch and said, "Please sign there on the sketch page. Where the knee is bending."

Hogan looked up and said, "There's not enough room. I

intended on writing you a nice note. There's not enough room on that page."

To which Nick leaned back with his arms in the air and replied, "Sign it anywhere you would like, Mr. Hogan."

Mr. Hogan started writing and Nick, unable to contain his excitement, craned forward to see what was being inscribed. Mr. Hogan continued writing, and then paused. "What's today?" he turned and asked me. Someone mentioned the day of the month. Mr. Hogan said, "No, what year?" At age 80, Mr. Hogan had arrived at a point where maybe the year was no longer important.

The meeting resumed. There were quite a few interesting technical exchanges, with Mr. Hogan providing many answers I had heard before. Other answers were fresh. At one point Nick asked, "Which were the important tournaments when you played?" In classic Hogan fashion, he answered with the response I had heard him give many times before: "Any that paid money."

Mr. Hogan elaborated that the more money the tournament paid, the more important it was to him. While many of today's players take the money for granted, back then the players didn't have the luxury and security of backup contracts to cover their expenses. Mr. Hogan then asked Nick what his next tournament was going to be. Nick said he was going to South Africa to play in the Sun City Million Dollar Classic. Hogan shook his head and said, "That's too far to go. But what's the purse size?"

When Nick said first prize was a million dollars, I thought Mr. Hogan was going to fall out of his chair. He was stunned at the answer. In fact, two other times during the meeting, out of the clear blue, Mr. Hogan looked at Nick and said, "You're going to play in South Africa for a million dollars first-place money?" He simply couldn't comprehend that figure. It was an arresting scene. Here was Faldo, a player who would give a million dollars or more for one U.S. Open medal, and there was Hogan, a man who possessed *five* U.S. Open medals who couldn't fathom winning a million dollars in one golf tournament.

The conversation turned to tournament preparation. Nick wanted to know Mr. Hogan's approach to handling pressure. Mr. Hogan told Nick he never played a competitive round where on each hole of the course he hadn't hit that shot before, even if he had only hit it in his mind. He explained that he never simply hit practice balls to work on swing mechanics while at a tournament site. His key thought was to mentally prepare for the tournament by playing the course in his mind. The purpose, he said, was to incorporate a belief system into his psyche. Even if he had never actually hit a particular shot on the course before, he wanted to feel he had. If he could remember the way a shot felt from his practice sessions, he could apply that feeling to the shot on the course.

This approach, said Mr. Hogan, enabled him to elevate his concentration and quiet his nerves. His method of displacing pressure was brilliant. Modern sports psychologists try all sorts of techniques to help players expel negative thoughts and replace them with positive imagery, but Mr. Hogan's approach was much simpler. All you had to do was *prepare*.

Mr. Hogan said, "Don't just hit practice balls. Hit the

9-iron into the back left corner past the bunker. Then remember what it felt like, so when you get to a shot and you need to make it, you already know what it feels like."

Nick asked Mr. Hogan what he thought was the most important shot in the game. "The driver," said Hogan, because the driver set up the hole and determined whether you could attack pins or were forced to play safely. Nick told Mr. Hogan that in today's game, fairway position wasn't very important. Players hit it so far and so high that there weren't any pins that could not be attacked. Hearing this, Hogan shook his head. The thought of shotmaking becoming obsolete, where the game came largely down to putting, was appalling to him. But, in the Majors, where shotmaking still rules, the driver is a player's most valued tool.

As the meeting drew to a close, Nick suggested I ask Mr. Hogan if we all could lunch together. I told Nick the offer would mean more coming from him. Nick seemed hesitant, but when he did ask, Mr. Hogan politely declined. Nick looked crushed, but David Hueber intervened and persuaded Mr. Hogan to adjourn to Shady Oaks.

At the club, Nick again asked Mr. Hogan if he wouldn't mind watching him hit a few shots after we ate. Mr. Hogan answered in a disarmingly polite way, "No, but thanks for asking." When Nick asked why not, Mr. Hogan jokingly said his eyes were so bad he couldn't see the ball in flight anyway. But then he explained that even if he watched Nick hit, he wouldn't say anything or make any comments. Nick assured him that was fine, hoping to persuade him to reconsider and come along. Mr. Hogan, however, politely said no.

To truly understand Mr. Hogan's answer you need only read his favorite saying, *The secret, the answers (to golf) are in the dirt.* That's how he wrote it. He wrote it on one of my favorite pictures he gave me. What he was saying is that you can't be taught belief in yourself. It must be learned through trial and error. When it really counts and you need that belief in yourself to succeed, it can only happen if you have dug it out of the dirt yourself.

Nick learned a lot about Mr. Hogan that day, especially his mental approach. When you spoke with Mr. Hogan, it often was necessary to read between the lines. By saying "no thanks" to the invitation to watch Nick hit balls, he was implying to Nick that he must acquire an indisputable belief in himself and his ability. There was no other way, and the opinion of others—Mr. Hogan included—was, in the final analysis, unimportant.

As we finished lunch, I suggested to Nick that he go up to the practice range and hit a few shots. It was my hope that David might talk Mr. Hogan into having a look at Nick's swing if Nick were at the driving range hitting shots. I sent a golf cart over to the 19th hole back door so David might be able to bring Mr. Hogan up and take a look. Nick got his clubs and hit balls briefly, but when we saw David moving up to the range by himself, we knew Mr. Hogan's decision not to watch Nick was final.

"I thought I had him for a minute," David explained. "I said, you know Mr. Hogan, Nick is up on the range hitting balls and after coming all the way from England, he really would appreciate it if you could watch him hit a few shots."

He said Mr. Hogan slowly raised his Chardonnay, took a sip and asked, "David, does he play our clubs?" David responded, "No, sir, he doesn't."

Mr. Hogan replied, "Then, I don't think so."

Hearing the exchange, Nick blurted, "Well, go down to the bloody pro shop and get me a set!" Nick made me promise that when he came to town again, that I'd have a set of Hogan clubs in a Hogan bag just in case. Then Nick asked me what it was that Mr. Hogan did with his swing. He said, "You saw him hit a lot of balls. What did you see?" I proceeded to give him the same lesson that Mr. Hogan had given me, including sharing the famous swing secret. It was an extraordinary moment for me: I was giving a swing lesson to the number one player in the world, and he was actually listening. My kids don't even listen to me.

My last memory of this fascinating encounter between two eerily similar players from completely different generations is of Nick and John at the airport. As I was walking out the terminal door back to my car, I turned to see Nick and John standing at the airline ticket counter, preparing to return to England. They were exchanging high-fives, filled to the brim with stories and memories to last a lifetime.

10

"Tonight's on Me"

MR. HOGAN'S LIFE away from the golf course followed identifiable patterns. Whereas most people incorporate some variations into their daily routine, Mr. Hogan was consistent about what time he went to the office, where he ate lunch, what he ate and drank, what time he practiced and how much he paid me for shagging balls. Whenever he strayed from his predictability, it was a surprise. And usually, a pleasant one.

Mr. Hogan arrived at his office at the Hogan Company at 8:45 each morning. There was a side door next to his parking space that opened directly into his office. It was like walking from your garage directly into your den at home. There were no wasted steps. This allowed him to get down to business without being interrupted by small talk. Once in the office, he seldom ventured out on the plant floor, instead choosing to rely on plant supervisors to keep him informed. The only place he visited regularly was the model shop, where the PGA staff players' equipment was assembled. He always kept close tabs on how these processes were handled.

There also was a routine to his appearance. Mr. Hogan

always wore a coat and tie, even when dress codes were re-laxed. He insisted that members of the Hogan Company sales group be well-appointed, too, especially on sales calls. He was a creature of habit who relied on a dry-cleaning es-tablishment in Dallas to deliver his clothes to his doorstep because they did the job the way he liked it done, even though he lived in west Fort Worth.

Upon completing duties at the plant, he would leave for Shady Oaks at 11:30 to have lunch. He then would either play or practice. Once lunch was over and the gangsome members headed to the golf course, Mr. Hogan went to the locker room and changed from his suit into his golf clothes to prac-tice. His golf dress was as fastidious as his off-course attire. Typically, he wore a Defini raglan sleeve shirt, slacks custom-made by a tailor in Fort Worth, his customary white Hogan cap, and if the weather was chilly, a cardigan sweater. Cash-mere only.

After he had practiced, he would sign my caddie ticket, a charge slip commonly used at country clubs. He paid me $7.50 for each session regardless of how long we worked. The amount he paid never wavered. The first time I worked for him he paid me $7.50, and four years later the fee remained $7.50. I never got a cost-of-living raise (I didn't complain).

The $7.50 he paid sure beat the 95 cents per hour Art paid me for working in the shop. Before I went out to shag balls with Mr. Hogan, I'd punch out on my time card. When we were finished, I punched back in. Art Hall saved himself $2.00 or $3.00 per day by having me do that. Those old pros never ceased to amaze me.

There were occasions when Mr. Hogan strayed from that $7.50 flat fee. One occasion is indelibly etched in my memory. One Friday afternoon, as Mr. Hogan was preparing to sign my caddie ticket, he looked up at me as I was standing on the opposite side of the counter and asked what my plans were for that evening. Now, why would Ben Hogan care what his shag boy was gonna do on a Friday night in Fort Worth, Texas? You can answer that one as well as I can. I'm sure I did a double take before I answered. But, it just so happened that I had a date that night. I was going to a movie and out for burgers at the local drive-thru.

Mr. Hogan stood there for a second and then asked me, "Is this a hot date?"

Again, I was a little taken aback. I answered, a little awkwardly, "I hope so."

He looked away from me and then down at the caddie ticket. To my amazement, he wrote down $15.00 instead of the usual $7.50. As he walked away, he said, "Tonight's on me."

Mr. Hogan didn't ask me all the time what I was doing on the weekend. Sometimes when he'd ask, I would tell him that I was staying home, hanging with the guys or going to play the front nine till dark. I think the fact that I was honest and never tried to take advantage of his generosity meant something to him.

Whenever Mr. Hogan is depicted as being so structured as to be cold and unfeeling, I reflect on that Friday afternoon. He had a distinctly human side. I could prove it, too, if only I'd thought to keep that $15.00 caddie ticket!

11

A Gift from Mr. Hogan

LIKE MANY YOUNGSTERS, my first clubs were not a formal set. None of my irons matched. While I did have a 2-iron through a pitching wedge, one was a MacGregor, another was a Wilson Staff and Dunlop made a third one. Few kids could afford to play golf at all, and the fact I had a full set was enough for me. When my cousin Al "Tuffy" Ochoa gave me his old set of MacGregor irons, I thought I had died and gone to heaven. That was the set I had when I began working at Shady Oaks.

A short time after I had started shagging balls for Mr. Hogan, he asked me what kind of clubs I was playing. I told him about my MacGregor irons. It was an innocent answer from a kid who didn't think forward enough that the guy asking the question might just own a golf club company. When we finished practicing and had walked back into the golf shop, Mr. Hogan asked if he could see my clubs. I readily complied. He pulled a couple of the irons from my bag and examined them closely.

He asked me if I liked them. I said that I did. He said he

liked the way they looked, walked out, and headed back to the locker room. When Mr. Hogan walked into the shop the next day he was carrying a box containing a set of irons. I assumed he was going to test some new clubs, which was normally the case. He walked up to me, didn't say anything and handed me the box. I took it and started walking out the door, intending to put the box on the cart with his bag. He stopped me before I reached the door.

"Where are you going?" he asked.

"I'm going to put the box on your cart," I replied, still not making much of the situation.

"Those are yours," he said. "See if you like them better than the MacGregors."

I looked over at Tom Sisolak, who was standing behind the counter. I didn't know who was more shocked—Tom or me. Here was my first set of brand-new irons, which would have been simply great in its own right. But they were given to me by none other than Ben Hogan, which was just a touch overwhelming for anyone, much less a teenage Mexican kid from Northside.

Our practice session that day was the longest two hours I ever spent with him. All I wanted to do was to try out my new clubs. When we were finally done, I jumped out on the range and started pounding balls. Knowing that no one had ever hit them before and seeing how shiny and new they were made me more excited than I had ever been before.

A couple of weeks later, Mr. Hogan and I were coming in from a practice session when he asked me how I liked my new clubs. I told him I thought they were terrific, and meant it. The next day, Mr. Hogan walked into the shop with a box of the same set of clubs he had given me. He handed them to me and instructed me to put them on his cart.

When I realized that this set was for him to hit, I was surprised—and a little impressed with myself. I was thinking, "Wow. He thought enough of my comment about the clubs that now he is going to try them."

It was customary for Mr. Hogan to test all club models manufactured by the Hogan Company. But he didn't actively play with the newest model introduced each year. For a long time he stayed with his original set, which was a 1954 Hogan model called the Personal blade. I believe he only used three sets competitively. His Precision model was his original blade made in 1953. From there, he switched to the 1954 Personal blade and then later moved on to the 1962 Power Thrust model.

We drove out to his favorite practice area by the 11th green. I jumped out of the cart, dumped his bag of balls on the ground and moved out to my usual spot. He opened the box and started hitting shots with some of the new clubs. When we had packed up and were headed back to the club-house, I asked him how he liked the new irons. In typical Hogan fashion he said, "They're not worth a shit." Mr. Hogan never did tell me why he didn't like them. Honestly, I didn't care. He wasn't getting mine back.

After I had been using the clubs for a few months, Mr. Hogan asked me if I still liked them. "I love them," I said. He asked me to show them to him. We walked back into the bag room, where he pulled one of the irons out and then another.

He looked down at one of the heads and said, "This club's got rust on it." I responded by saying that was okay. I could use steel wool and wipe the clubhead and remove that. Without missing a step, Mr. Hogan then turned, walked over to the shop counter and reached for the phone.

I could tell by bits of the conversation he had called the Hogan plant. I stood nearby and heard him ask for Archie Allision, the account sales rep who took care of our Hogan orders at Shady Oaks. A few seconds went by and then he said, "Archie, I'm standing in the golf shop, I have Jody's 7-iron in my hand and it's got rust on it."

I thought, *Oh, no!*

Now, Archie was a terrific guy. Anyone who met him immediately liked him. I suddenly thought, *Great, I've gotten Archie in trouble.* I had no idea why. After all, it was just a little rust spot. Mr. Hogan didn't say another word. He hung up the phone and sat on the stool waiting for Archie. Ten minutes later, Archie came trotting up the path to the golf shop, walked in the door, and came face to face with Mr. Hogan, who was still sitting on the stool waiting. Me, I was back in the bag room at the workbench out of the way, but close enough to see when Archie arrived.

Mr. Hogan handed him the 7-iron and showed him the rust. To his credit, Archie didn't offer any excuses. He took the club, looked it over and told Mr. Hogan that he would take care of it. With that, Mr. Hogan walked out, heading back to the grillroom. As soon as Mr. Hogan was a step out the door, I started to apologize to Archie big time. He patiently calmed me down and assured me it was no big deal. He explained that every now and then a set wasn't chromed properly and rust appeared. To be sure the whole set was okay, Archie took the other clubs as well. I thought, great, the crisis was over.

A couple of days later, Archie showed up at the shop with my irons. They looked brand-new. Instead of only re-chroming the 7-iron, he had re-chromed the entire set. I was shocked, thanking him and apologizing in the same breath. When Mr. Hogan came out to the club that afternoon, he asked me if I had talked to Archie and if I'd received another set. I happily reported that Archie had indeed taken care of me and that the clubs looked great.

Just to reassure him, I walked back to my bag, grabbed the infamous 7-iron, and brought it back to show him. As I handed him the club, I said, "They look brand-new."

Wrong comment! Mr. Hogan looked at me with a confused expression on his face and said, "Look brand-new? What did Archie do? Didn't he bring you a new set?" I quickly explained that Archie had stripped and re-chromed the whole set to make sure the others didn't rust. Immediately, Mr. Hogan was back on the phone to the plant, asking for Archie. When Mr. Hogan hung up the telephone, he called for me (I was hiding in the bag room) and told me to come find him when Archie got to the golf shop.

In record time Archie arrived and walked through the door carrying a box of irons, which I soon found out were to replace the ones he had re-chromed for me. I started my "I'm sorry" routine and then went to the grill for Mr. Hogan. Archie waited in the shop, and Lord only knows what was going through his mind.

Mr. Hogan and I came back into the golf shop, and he walked up to Archie and asked why the clubs were re-chromed. Before Archie could offer an answer, Mr. Hogan stated that the Hogan Company did not re-chrome irons because it changed the swing weight. This meant the clubs would never match up. Archie was really sweating it at that point. He apologized and said that he had heard Mr. Hogan wrong the first time and thought he merely wanted the clubs redone, not replaced. Mr. Hogan turned and left.

To Archie's credit, this incident never affected our relationship. We've laughed about it several times through the years. It was a telling glimpse into Mr. Hogan's personal view of perfection. When you think about all the clubs designed by all the great players over the years, and the legends who have lent their names to them—Jones, Nelson, Hagen, Palmer, Nicklaus and others—only Mr. Hogan's clubs are so synonymous with quality as to have survived the test of time.

12

The Price of a Signature

MR. HOGAN RARELY MADE public appearances, and those he did make were guarded. He never quite comprehended why the American public adored him, and his desire for privacy usually won out over requests to speak or attend banquets. Yet, he did understand the significance and value of an item with his signature on it.

That knowledge coupled with his generous tendency to support a good cause prompted Mr. Hogan to sign items for charity. Early on, his personal secretary, Claribel Kelly, established a simple but efficient cataloguing system to record what pieces were signed, who they were for and how many were fulfilled. Even after he was finished playing competitively, Mr. Hogan received up to 2,000 autograph requests per week. At one point they added a staff person just to track the requests. With that, the only sure way to get his autograph was to know someone who had direct access to him. I filled this role from time to time. I could walk in, sit for a few minutes and get him to sign something—if he deemed it worthy of signing.

≈ III ≈

One request seemed particularly worthwhile. A friend of mine, Lee Davis, had a friend who was serving on the Orange County (California) Special Olympics Committee. He informed me that a benefit auction was scheduled prior to the upcoming competitions, and asked if I could have Mr. Hogan sign a beautiful print created by artist Alan Zuniga. Lee added that the tournament chairman, Eddie Chevalier, would be especially appreciative if I could deliver the request. Eddie had a daughter who had died recently, and she had participated in a past Special Olympics event. I promised to see what I could do.

Mr. Hogan was in his 80s by this time and had cut back dramatically on the number of items he signed. His health wasn't good and he visited the office less frequently. Nevertheless, I felt comfortable imposing on him. When I explained to Mr. Hogan that the prints would help raise money for the Special Olympics, he was more than happy to sign them. When he saw the print, he was pleased with the artist's depiction of him. He was rarely pleased with renderings of his likeness, but this one—a collage of Mr. Hogan in various stages of the swing, with a bust portrait in the center—pleased him very much. "That does look like me," he said to Mrs. Hogan.

Mr. Hogan signed the prints readily and kept the one offered to him. A few weeks later, my morning mail contained an appreciative letter from Eddie Chevalier with a copy of his thank-you letter to Mr. Hogan. Eddie noted that the print drew a winning bid of $7,700—an extraordinary sum, considering this was the Special Olympics, not Sotheby's. A short time later, Eddie himself called me to say thanks again, and to ask for one more favor: Would I ask Mr. Hogan to accept, as a token of Eddie's heartfelt thanks, the last gold medal his daughter won in the Special Olympics competition before she passed away?

I was stunned by Eddie's gesture, but after considering it briefly, told him I would pass on his request of asking Mr. Hogan to accept the medal. Knowing Mr. Hogan, I couldn't imagine that he would accept it. Especially something so cherished and deeply personal as that medal.

The next time I went to see Mr. Hogan, some time had passed since he had signed the Zuniga print. I asked him if he remembered it, and he said he did. I then told Mr. Hogan of Eddie's request to give him his daughter's gold medal.

Mr. Hogan leaned forward as though he hadn't heard me correctly. When the words sank in, our eyes met for the longest time. He didn't say anything. Clearly, Mr. Hogan could not grasp how powerful his personage was, or comprehend his capacity to affect people so deeply.

As was often his reaction to something incomprehensible, Mr. Hogan did not use words to express what he was thinking or feeling. He didn't say whether I was right or wrong in telling Eddie to keep his daughter's medal. In fact, Mr. Hogan didn't say anything. He simply dropped his head and shook it slowly from side to side in wonder and disbelief.

13

Mr. Hogan on Golf:
Playing Theories from the Legend

THROUGH HIS MANY HOURS of practice and his many hours of competition, Mr. Hogan developed several playing theories that worked well for him. While some of the theories will ring true and work for golfers of all abilities, some will only apply to him because of his unique talent and tendencies. He also had a few unique theories about life in general that give further insight into his personality on the course and off.

HIT LONG IRONS HIGH, SHORT IRONS LOW

ONE OF MR. HOGAN's most important ball-striking theories pertained to ball flight. It had more to do with the ball's trajectory, or height, than it did curvature. On iron shots especially, he felt that having firm command over trajectory optimized his chances of hitting the ball a precise distance. His first thought was always, "How high should the ball fly?"

Mr. Hogan told me it was best to hit the long irons—the 4-, 3- and 2-iron—as high as possible. The chief benefit was distance control; he knew that once the ball reached the apex of its flight, it would fall out of the sky rather than run an indeterminate distance along the ground. The drawback, he admitted, was direction control. The higher you hit the ball, the more it was at the mercy of the wind and could be blown off-line. On balance, however, he felt distance control was more important.

The short irons—the 8- and 9-irons, pitching wedge and sand wedge—Mr. Hogan felt should be hit low. The low trajectory meant they came into the green with a great deal of speed, but he had marvelous control over the way they reacted after landing. Generally, he spun the ball a great deal. His shots would skip twice and stop immediately. Many players today do not opt for this strategy. They feel a high shot that lands softly and settles quickly is the best option regardless of the club in hand. But they do not control spin the way Mr. Hogan did. He had a knack for reducing backspin when necessary, and applying more when the occasion called for it. By hitting the ball low, he kept it underneath the wind and thus had more command over the distance the ball flew.

Overclub When Playing Downwind

When the wind was up, Mr. Hogan believed you should hit the ball low regardless of which direction it was blowing. Obviously, you want to keep the ball low if the wind is blowing against you and in many cases you want a low trajectory if the wind is blowing from the left or right. But his belief that you should keep the ball low when it is blowing with you was his alone. The reasoning, when one examines it closely, makes a great deal of sense.

When you're playing downwind, the ball rarely flies as high as it would normally. The wind tends to flatten the shot out, and it comes into the green on a hard, flat trajectory that is difficult to control. Mr. Hogan felt that by taking a club with less loft, the ball flew low on its own accord and was not exacerbated by the wind. It's an effective technique. If you're playing a shot in windy conditions that would normally be an 8-iron for you on a calm day, you might consider taking a 7-iron instead and making a softer swing. It's a win-win scenario. You control the direction better and have a far better chance of judging the distance as well.

PLAY FULL SHOTS TO FRONT PINS, THREE-QUARTER SHOTS TO BACK PINS

ANOTHER HOGAN BASIC CONCEPT was to play full shots to pins located on the front of the green, but to swing at 75 percent capacity when the flagstick was on the back of the green. It's an advanced strategy, but one you should employ as your skill level increases.

Again, it all has to do with control. Mr. Hogan felt that full shots are easier to hit a precise distance. When the flag is positioned at the front of the green, coming up just short of the green can leave you with a tricky chip, which could happen on a less than full swing attempt. But, if the player made a full swing and he misjudged the shot and hit the ball farther than expected, he at least would still be putting. This didn't mean that if he judged the shot as a normal 8-iron that he would hit a hard 9-iron instead. He simply chose the club that would assure him of reaching the front of the green at worst, and pin high at best. Something a bit long was acceptable.

Conversely, he liked to hit three-quarter shots to a pin on the back of the green. That's because a three-quarter shot, if it is misjudged, more often than not comes up short. As Hogan saw it, a less than exact swing would still leave the ball on the green, just short of the pin, with an uphill putt—the easiest kind. His goal was to remove any possibility of the ball going over the green, which would leave a tough downhill chip. So, if the shot yardage called for a hard 8-iron or maybe a softer 7-iron, he'd hit the 7-iron with less than full effort, thereby increasing his chances of putting for a birdie.

This strategy also applies to the accomplished player. The fact is, most everyday amateurs habitually underclub. Mr. Hogan's concept is based on the assumption that you know how far you can hit each iron in your bag.

AIM AT TROUBLE, CURVE BALL AWAY FROM IT

MR. HOGAN BELIEVED the best way to protect against hitting into trouble was to confront the trouble head on. This meant you had to take control of your shot and use the hazard as your target. His belief was to play at the trouble rather than aiming away from it. This strategy is terrifying to mere mortals, but Mr. Hogan played with ironclad assurance that he could aim at a bunker, water hazard or even out-of-bounds and easily move the ball away from it. He was the original "have-no-fear" player. His swing didn't double-cross him and leave the ball where he didn't want it, which is to say he wasn't mortal in that regard.

His victory at Carnoustie in the 1953 British Open produced a prime example of how he exercised this logic. The 6th hole at Carnoustie is a 575-yard par 5 with a bunker complex just to the left of where you would normally aim your tee shot. Farther to the left, beyond the bunkers, is a 25-yard strip of fairway which is perilously close to the out-of-bounds that runs the entire length of the hole. The out-of-bounds is marked by a fence, painted a brilliant white that almost screams of the danger. Visually, it is one of the most intimidating shots in all of golf.

Strategically, the hole is vexing. If the player gambles for that 25-yard landing area and succeeds, he is rewarded with a much shorter approach shot into the green plus he avoids playing over the small hazard that protects the green from the right side. But if he pulls the shot or hooks it just a bit, disaster occurs. The ball is out-of-bounds! The safe play— and the one the vast majority of players opt for—is the wide landing area to the right of the bunker complex (it's where we mortals aim).

This compact area between the out-of-bounds and the bunker complex is known today as Hogan's Alley after the way Mr. Hogan played the hole in that British Open. Each of the four rounds that year, he went for that narrow strip of fairway. Each day, he hit his target. He *knew* he could hit the shot at that devilish white fence and move the ball away from it. And he played the hole under par for the championship.

Visually, the hole is so intimidating you must see it to believe it. The first time I played Carnoustie, in 1988, I came away with a full appreciation for the strength of character Mr. Hogan displayed in playing it the way he did. The round started off wonderfully. I birdied the second, fourth and fifth holes, and arrived at the fabled sixth hole three under par to boot. My companion, Ken Smith, and I were the only ones in sight on this calm, beautiful late afternoon. I was taking in everything about the sixth hole and was determined to play my tee shot to Hogan's Alley. After all, I had told him I was going there. I wanted to report back that in all things, I had hit "his" shot there.

I teed up my ball and took dead aim down the left side of the hole, glancing over my left shoulder at that white fence marking the out-of-bounds. I started my backswing and swung at the ball. Just before impact, I flinched, mentally and physically. I blocked the ball way to the right, where it landed safely on the right side of the fairway. I was stunned. It was a meaningless round of golf, and I still couldn't release the club and hit the shot into Hogan's Alley. My mind wouldn't let me do it—the out-of-bounds was too much to handle. How could he have done it under all that pressure? I wish I had asked, but I already knew the answer.

And, yes, I did tell him about the shot when I returned home. We had a good laugh!

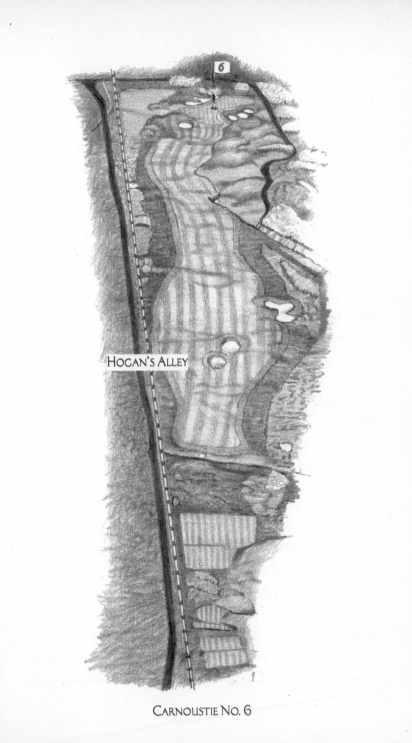

Hogan's Alley

Carnoustie No. 6

BE AWARE OF THE "SMALL CLUB" PHENOMENON

THE CONCEPT OF FEEL is extraordinary and problematic to contemplate and discuss. Trying to articulate how to hit a soft 7-iron or a hard 8-iron is extremely difficult, if not impossible to teach. Feel is ephemeral and difficult to impart. Yet it is vital if one is to play the game with any proficiency. The distance a golfer needs to hit the ball rarely fits into what constitutes a normal swing speed. To some degree he must swing the club faster or slower to accommodate that distance. Detecting that speed is instinctive, almost innate.

In analyzing this whole concept of feel, it must be understood that the hands are the major component. To hit the in-between shot, a player goes at it hard or backs off. It is the hands that perform this minor addition or subtraction of effort.

As you can imagine, Mr. Hogan fielded a slew of questions on many aspects of the game, and was often asked to go into great detail. In regard to feel, he went to great lengths to explain how the club feels in your hands. What he said had little to do with swing mechanics if you listened closely. It was explicitly clear that Mr. Hogan's greatest talent was his wonderful sense of feel.

Mr. Hogan believed that when he was playing well, the club felt *smaller* in his hands. He couldn't explain why the club felt smaller on some days than others, but he said it was a fact nonetheless. After hearing that, I never built up another grip. I keep them as small as I can, knowing that a smaller grip transmits the weight of the club, and the feeling of impact, better than one with a larger diameter.

A friend told me that Tommy John, a four-time All-Star pitcher who retired with 288 career wins, once visited Shady Oaks for a round of golf. When Mr. Hogan met Tommy, he asked him, "When you were really throwing the ball well, how did the ball feel? Smaller?" Tommy said yes, which satisfied Mr. Hogan.

So, lose the oversized grips!

GRIP THE CLUB PROPERLY

IT'S OFTEN BEEN SAID that making even a slight change in your grip is the single most difficult thing to do in competitive golf. Golfers of all abilities fight anyone who asks them to change their grip, and alter it only with great reluctance and solid assurance that the change is for the better.

A couple of years ago, I was in Los Angeles at Bel-Air Country Club watching my friend Lee Davis compete in an interclub match that coincidentally was held during the week of the Los Angeles Open. While waiting for play to start, I stopped in the grill for a cup of coffee. I took a seat at a table with a group of people that included Ken Venturi, the 1964 U.S. Open champion and veteran television golf analyst.

The conversation turned to how a player gripped the club. Venturi said that after playing a round of golf with Byron Nelson one day, Nelson suggested that he change his grip. Ken said that he made the change, but that it took two years for the somewhat simple-looking change to take hold. Ken lamented that it was the single most difficult change to his swing he had ever made. Many golfers would agree with that. The grip is that crucial. It has to have the right feel.

Mr. Hogan's grip was a standard overlapping Vardon grip, in which the little finger of the right hand rests atop the left index finger. Mr. Hogan made one slight variation to it. He moved the little finger of his right hand into the space between the left index finger and the middle finger rather than resting it atop the index finger. This wasn't a big deal. His grip was very natural and comfortable looking, as if he were born with it there.

Still, no doubt because of Mr. Hogan's ball-striking abilities, many people thought there was something a little different with his grip—a secret, perhaps. Some people even went to the length of asking Mr. Hogan about his grip. One day at Shady Oaks while he was signing my caddie ticket, a member walked up and said, "Ben, I need to ask you a question about your grip." Mr. Hogan turned and said sure.

The member asked why Mr. Hogan made that slight variation in his grip. Mr. Hogan considered the question thoughtfully. He raised his hands up in front of his face and moved the little finger on his right hand back and forth, placing it on top and between those on his left hand. This took a minute or so. I thought to myself, *I can't wait to hear this answer.* And then he replied, "If I leave the little finger on top of the left index finger to hit shots, the left index finger is gonna hurt. I don't see any reason to hurt my finger just to hit the ball." I'm sure that was not the technical response the member was searching for. I was a little disappointed myself. But, as Mr. Hogan simply pointed out, there was no technical reason for it. It was all about feel.

LOYALTY ABOVE ALL ELSE

IN 1994, NICK FALDO WAS WRITING his instructional book, *Faldo: A Swing for Life*. He asked me to approach Mr. Hogan about writing the foreword to the book. I told Nick I'd ask, even though I didn't recall ever seeing a foreword written by Mr. Hogan.

I told Nick to write out some notes about what he thought Mr. Hogan could say and send it to me. I knew there wasn't a chance in hell that Mr. Hogan was going to write something on his own. Nick faxed me a short page with remarks for the foreword.

After reading the remarks, I called Nick and said Mr. Hogan would never agree to some of the wording on the fax. For example, a reference to Mr. Hogan as "being one of the greatest players ever to live" was something I knew he wouldn't go along with. I asked Nick to let me take a stab, and I'd fax him my notes. I did this, and we came up with something agreeable.

I called Mr. Hogan's office and talked to Mrs. Hogan. I asked her if she could set aside some time for me to relay a favor that Nick wanted to ask of Mr. Hogan. She told me to come on over to the office. When I arrived, Pat Martin, the secretary who had taken over for Doxie Williams, greeted me and called for Mrs. Hogan. I took a couple of minutes with Mrs. Hogan by herself to explain exactly what Nick wanted. Since she was receptive to the idea, we both went into Mr. Hogan's office to talk with him.

After handing Mr. Hogan a copy of the foreword I had written, Mrs. Hogan asked me to read it to him. (He was having trouble with his eyesight.) I read the foreword while Mr. Hogan listened intently. It took only a minute or so to read the passage. When I finished, Mrs. Hogan surprised me by saying that she thought the foreword was nicely written and Ben should sign it. But Mr. Hogan looked over to me and said, "Jody, tell Nick I very much appreciate him asking, but I can't do it."

Mr. Hogan explained to Mrs. Hogan and me that he couldn't sign the foreword because he didn't know Nick very well. To my surprise, Mrs. Hogan argued back by saying that Nick was a fine English boy and a champion just like Ben. One of her comments was that Nick probably had ideas about golf that people wanted to hear, just as Ben had views that helped the golfing public. I assumed she was referring to Mr. Hogan's *Five Lessons* book.

Mr. Hogan listened intently, but he argued back that he didn't know what Nick believed or didn't believe about golf. Then, he said forcefully, "Valerie, I'm not gonna read the damn book." This was his final answer. I just sat, watched and said nothing. Finally, I started to get up. But when Mr. Hogan looked over at me, I realized he wasn't finished.

Mr. Hogan turned his attention to me and said, "Jody, I can't sign that because it would be a slap in the face to all the

American boys who over the years have asked me the very same thing and I told them no. I would never show that kind of disrespect to those boys."

I can guarantee you that Mr. Hogan had no idea who "those boys" were. I could have asked him for a name, and he wouldn't have been able to give me one. But to Ben Hogan, the names didn't matter. He simply remembered that other golfers at different points in the past had asked him for the same favor and they were Americans. He would not cross that line.

I nodded in full agreement and looked over to Mrs. Hogan who had nothing else to say. The meeting was over. In the end, it had all come down to Mr. Hogan's personal sense of loyalty.

THE IMPORTANCE OF QUALITY

WHEN MR. HOGAN WAS IN CHARGE of his plant's operations, one of his little-known demands was that all PGA tour staff equipment was assembled with pins inserted in the hosel portion of each iron head. The pins were used to fasten the shaft and clubhead together, thus ensuring a club would remain intact. The epoxy glue used in the 1950s and 1960s was not very reliable. In those days seeing a clubhead come loose and fly off was not unusual. A bad epoxy mix would reveal itself at the worst of times.

Long after the quality of epoxy improved and the rest of the golf industry stopped fastening the head to the shaft with pins, Mr. Hogan kept doing it. Eventually he used epoxy only for the sets he sold commercially, but well into the 1980s he continued pinning the clubheads of the clubs used by tour players. He did not want to risk having a player's clubhead fly off in the heat of battle. It wasn't necessary, but he did it anyway. To Mr. Hogan, quality and dependability were everything—especially if his name was involved.

THE MEDIA IS NOT YOUR FRIEND

MR. HOGAN DID NOT CARE for the media, especially in his later years. He once did an ESPN interview, and he considered it a disaster. When he saw the video, he was embarrassed and said he looked awkward. He said he'd never do another interview.

Although he liked some members of the media personally, he didn't feel he could trust them in general. Mrs. Hogan offered an explanation to me as to why he felt the way he did. She said that in the early 1950s Ben had become friendly with one writer, who even traveled extensively with them. This writer rode in the motorcade during the famous New York City ticker tape parade in 1953 after Mr. Hogan completed the Triple Crown with his victory in the British Open. But the writer betrayed their trust. He took what they told him, distorted it and sensationalized it. The publicity-shy Hogans never looked at the media the same way after that.

Mr. Hogan did, at one point, think about writing an autobiography. He even asked Herbert Warren Wind, who was the coauthor of the *Five Lessons* book, if he would be interested in doing it. Wind declined. Mr. Hogan never asked anybody else because he didn't know any other writers well enough to trust them. The only writer Doxie said the Hogans might have trusted was Dan Jenkins, a fine golf writer who also was from Fort Worth and knew the Hogans well. But they weren't sure that Dan's writing style would capture them the way they wanted. If only Jenkins had known.

In a conversation with Nick Faldo in 1992, Mr. Hogan relayed to Nick his feelings about dealing with the media. Nick asked him, "Mr. Hogan, how do you deal with the media?" His reply was, "I don't talk to them." Upon hearing that, Nick turned to his agent, John Simpson, and said, "I told you we shouldn't talk to them. I'm not going to anymore." Of course, in this day and age it is impossible for Nick to follow Mr. Hogan's advice.

Thank goodness he and others don't.

14

Proverbial Hogan

So many anecdotes involving Mr. Hogan end with a terse payoff line that startles or provokes. Knowing him as I did, however, I appreciate just as much the softer, slice-of-life episodes recounted by people who had occasion to meet Mr. Hogan personally. The following tales are not uncommonly dramatic, but grow a bit richer each time I hear them. Like stories in the Bible, each contains a parable. Mr. Hogan rarely told the whole story, very often leaving his audience to extract the full meaning for themselves.

THE OUT-OF-TOWN GUY

Every golfer has experienced the out-of-town guy. He's the fellow who shows up wanting to join the "big game," and making as persuasive an argument as possible that he deserves inclusion. One day, the out-of-town guy showed up to play in the Shady Oaks gangsome on a day Mr. Hogan had decided to play. This guy, who was loud and friendly, was paired with Mr. Hogan.

The gangsome was uncommonly disorganized that day. The pairings were shuffled and reshuffled and I scrambled about the first tee switching bags from cart to cart. As there wasn't much play outside the gangsome, Art Hall invited me to jump on a cart with him and watch Mr. Hogan play a few holes.

We caught his foursome on the tee at No. 6, a good par 4 with trees lining both sides of the fairway. Mr. Hogan hit his tee shot right center in the fairway, leaving himself 150 yards to the green. The out-of-town guy hit his tee shot on the same line and a few steps past Mr. Hogan's ball. As Mr. Hogan was away, he played to the green first. He chose a 7-iron. His ball landed about 10 feet left of the pin. Immediately, the out-of-town guy asked, "What club did you hit?"

Mr. Hogan, who had reached down to pick up his cigarette, tossed it back to the ground. He asked the caddie for another ball and took another club. He surprisingly hit another shot, which landed just to the right of the hole. He handed the club to the caddie, took a third ball and pulled another club. He hit again, and this shot landed just left of the hole and past it.

Mr. Hogan's answer to the out-of-town guy, who must have been annoying Mr. Hogan with various chitchat before we got there, was: "I hit an 8, a 7 and a 6." The out-of-town guy just stood there with his mouth open. Mr. Hogan did not like anyone looking in his bag to see what club he'd hit or anyone asking him what club he'd hit.

The guest was in for more on the eighth hole, a 615-yard par 5, which bends to the right around a fairway bunker and a thickly populated grove of huge, live oak trees. The normal tee shot is a driver left of the bunker. To hit your ball over the bunker would take a big drive, since the carry is about 280 yards.

But back then, there was another route less taken. If you looked closely, you saw a 15-yard gap within the canopies of the live oaks. There are houses in that area today, but back then it was only trees and knee-deep grass. It was a narrow opening, but if you squeezed a ball through it, you could cut the dogleg—and shorten the hole—in a major way. It really was a "sucker" tee shot. If you missed and hit the trees, you were dead.

Mr. Hogan teed his ball, addressed it with purpose and ripped it right through the gap. I think the round was over right then and there for the out-of-town guy. I'm sure he considered the same strategy, but he didn't have the courage. He played the rest of the round in respectful silence. That's how Ben Hogan used to take care of the out-of-town guys—all action, few words.

MR. BEMAN COMES UP EMPTY

I ONCE HAD A TROUBLING SPELL where I hit a lot of double-cross shots. I would position myself to hit a left-to-right fade, and for whatever reason, out of the blue I'd hit a right-to-left hook instead. I was in Palm Springs, California, at the

time and so was Lee Trevino. I'd known Lee since the early
'60s. At wits end, I asked him for help. He couldn't have been
nicer. He explained the cause of the double-cross as well as
the solution. It worked like a charm.

Some time later, I repeated Lee's swing secret to a fellow
who also was plagued by the double-cross. When this fellow
ran into Lee, he made a point of telling Lee how much he
appreciated his swing secret, even though it came from me.
Well, Lee was not at all happy that I had shared his hard-
earned finding with someone without asking for permission
first. Lee told me pointedly, "I worked hard to figure that out.
Don't go around giving it to them. Let them do their own
work."

So, Mr. Hogan was not the only man who carefully guarded
his knowledge about golf. In truth, many self-made players who
solved golf's complexities were very selective about who they
chose to enlighten. An exchange between Deane Beman, the
first commissioner of the PGA Tour, and Mr. Hogan pointed
this out emphatically.

Beman had flown into Fort Worth for a meeting with
Mr. Hogan. Beman didn't arrive with an agenda; it was more
of a courtesy visit. David Hueber, the president of the Hogan
Company, sat in on the meeting and told me the conversation
that day went in many directions. One of the topics was golf
balls and how to make a ball do this or that, depending on
the ball's construction.

It's important to note that the conversation took place
in the early 1990s, when every good player embraced the wound,
three-piece ball. The general consensus was that solid balls,

which were more durable but hard as rocks, were for women, old men and poor golfers who couldn't play the wound ball for two holes without putting a gash in the cover.

David said that at one point in the conversation, Mr. Hogan leaned back, thought about the matter, and said, "If I had my choice of balls, I'd play a solid ball instead of a wound ball." Both Hueber and Beman were shocked by what Mr. Hogan said. Here was the game's greatest ball-striker, who would only play with forged irons and persimmon woods, and presumably a softer ball he could spin more and control better, saying he preferred a solid ball.

Beman, of course, immediately fired back, "Why?"

Mr. Hogan looked at him and said, "I'm not going to tell you."

The terseness of the answer explains why some people viewed Mr. Hogan as self-centered and even rude. But there is another way to look at it. If Mr. Hogan told Beman why he preferred the solid ball, Beman would have wanted to discuss the subject further. Mr. Hogan viewed the ensuing give-and-take as having no value. It was enough that he considered his point of view before expressing it, and in the end his answer was good enough for him. His philosophy was, "I've figured it out. Now you go do the same."

Mr. Hogan certainly was consistent. His answers to questions about the golf swing were usually just as clipped. He felt that the only way a person could arrive at an answer that had any personal meaning was by obtaining that answer on his own.

As for his opinion on the solid ball, my guess is that it

had to do with feel. Hogan was the quintessential feel player his entire career. Then in his 80s, he derived more emphatic feedback from a solid ball.

But it's only a guess. Like Deane Beman, I'll have to sort it out on my own.

THE HARDEST PAR 3 IN THE WORLD

AS I PLAYED a great deal of competitive golf on some very fine courses, I often was asked if I knew Mr. Hogan's opinion of certain holes. Usually I couldn't give a very satisfying answer. Mr. Hogan was reluctant to praise a course or individual hole too lavishly, fearing his answer might be construed as offensive to another course.

For many years, I played in the Anderson Invitational at Winged Foot in New York. I had a friend who said someone had told him that Mr. Hogan thought the 10th hole on the west course there was the best par 3 he ever played. I was curious if it was true, and asked Hank Rojas, who worked in public relations and advertising for the Hogan Company, to ask Mr. Hogan. I didn't want to make a trip to the plant for one question.

Hank posed the question to Mr. Hogan and reported to me that Mr. Hogan said it was one of the best holes he had played and that he liked it. Judging by the brevity of the response, however, Mr. Hogan clearly didn't think this was the best he had ever played. Otherwise he would have said so.

A short time later, while at Pinehurst preparing for the

North-South Amateur, I fell into a conversation about Winged Foot's 10th hole with John Collier, a Shady Oaks member. John had spoken with Mr. Hogan sometime previous, and said Mr. Hogan told him the sixth hole on Pinehurst's No. 2 course was the hardest par 3 to birdie he had ever played. Mr. Hogan told John the back-left pin placement was impossible to get close to.

The sixth hole measures 212 yards and has a large sand bunker to the left of the green and a couple of bunkers on the right. The domed-shaped green has severe drop-offs at the front and rear. The putting surface is undulating; there isn't a straight putt of more than two feet on the entire green. Playing the sixth hole in practice with John that day, we agreed with Mr. Hogan. The only thought in my mind was par it. I heard Jimmy Demaret once say that you should always try to birdie a par 3, even at the expense of making a bogey, because it's the easiest way to gain a shot on the tournament field. I'm not sure Mr. Demaret was thinking of this hole when he said that.

So you want to play the PGA Tour

I can't count how many times Mr. Hogan was asked whether he thought a certain player could make it on the PGA Tour. His standard response was: "I would not try to play the tour unless I could guarantee myself I could hit every fairway and 18 greens each and every round I played."

At first listen, Mr. Hogan's statement sounds ridiculous.

Nobody hits every fairway and every green. But remember what I said about Mr. Hogan speaking in parables. Mr. Hogan was literal. He didn't say you *had* to hit 18 greens. He said you should know you *could* hit 18 greens. There's a marked difference. The statement, rephrased, might read, "If a player has the skill and talent to hit 18 greens and every fairway on a given day, then on the whole he may be good enough to give the tour a try."

DON'T SPEAK TOO SOON

ONE YEAR, MR. HOGAN PLAYED in the Big Brothers of Fort Worth Charity Golf Tournament, which raised funds to support the local chapter. It was a one-day pro-am held at Ridglea Country Club's south course on a sunny, windy fall day.

A couple of us left the golf shop to watch Mr. Hogan play. On the 11th hole, Mr. Hogan's tee shot was dead center of the fairway about 160 yards out. Because this was primarily an exhibition, ropes didn't restrain the gallery. Instead they formed a semicircle around Mr. Hogan as he prepared to play his approach shot to the upper part of the two-tiered green.

There was a blustery wind blowing straight into Mr. Hogan's face. After much consideration, he pulled out a 4-iron. He addressed his ball, waggled the club and let it fly. His shot came off the clubface very low and straight as an arrow toward the flag. Suddenly, a woman in the gallery blurted, "He bladed it!" Mr. Hogan never took his eyes off his shot.

I immediately turned to face the woman, whom I recognized as a member's wife from Shady Oaks. I turned back to see the ball land on the green's bottom tier. It struck the green with a skidding action and jumped immediately onto the top tier. It looked like the ball was going to hit the flagstick, but instead crept past it. When the ball stopped, it was about five feet past the pin. It was a fantastic-looking shot that provoked applause and a few excited cheers.

By Mr. Hogan's initial reaction, I didn't think he had heard the woman. But then with the shot perfectly settled on the green, he turned around. Mr. Hogan stared at her for what seemed like forever. She must have felt she was turning to salt, especially since they probably knew each other. Nobody moved. He didn't say a word. Yet again, he didn't need to use words when his actions spoke clearly for him.

WOE TO HE WHO DRAWS THE BALL

FROM TIME TO TIME, Mark O'Meara used to stop in at Shady Oaks and ask Mr. Hogan for help. Since Mark was a Hogan staff player and played their equipment, he had access to Mr. Hogan. In 1987, Mark arrived for the Colonial Tournament. He drove over to visit Mr. Hogan after the Wednesday pro-am round. This was the year that O'Meara was starting to emerge as an elite player. He was clearly at the top of his game and had won several tournaments.

Mark went to the range to hit some shots, and Mr.

Hogan followed a short time later. Mark's natural shot is a draw, and Mr. Hogan took exception to it. After watching a couple of balls start to the right and then hook back to the target, Mr. Hogan said: "I never saw a great player that hit only a hook." This meant he never saw a great player who hit a hook as his basic shot.

Mark promptly shot 80 in the first round, and the next day took the first airplane out of town. Rumor around the shop was Mark spent the first round trying to play a fade instead of his natural draw.

NEXT CASE!

AFTER FRED COUPLES WON the 1992 Masters, *Golf World* carried a wonderful action photograph of him swinging his driver with his hands extended two feet past impact.

What makes the photo so intriguing and memorable is that his right hand has come totally off the grip. David Hueber was curious as to what Mr. Hogan's reaction to that swing photo would be. He walked into Mr. Hogan's office and handed him the magazine. Hogan took it, studied the photo and asked: "Who's this?"

"That's Freddie Couples," replied David. "He just won the Masters and is the leading money winner on tour this year. Did you notice his right hand is off the club?"

Mr. Hogan replied, "He must not need it there."

QUESTION AND ANSWER

WILLI HOFFMAN, A GERMAN PRO who is a friend of Bern-
hard Langer's, met Mr. Hogan through his friendship with
Peter Kostis, the golf announcer and instructor. In 1984, Willi
traveled with Kostis to Fort Worth, where Peter had scheduled an interview with Mr. Hogan. Peter was on an assign-
ment for *Golf Digest* to gather material from Hogan for an
upcoming edition of the magazine.

The first part of the interview was scheduled for Mr.
Hogan's office at the old Pafford Street plant. Mr. Hogan
agreed to allow Willi to attend, so long as he did not ask any
questions. The meeting got under way with Kostis and Mr.
Hogan talking softly. Willi was seated some distance away. English is not his first language, and with their voices muted,
it meant Willi couldn't discern much of what was being discussed. Willi became more and more anxious by the minute,
but adhered to his "gag order" and said nothing. The interview concluded after 30 minutes.

Next, the three men moved from Mr. Hogan's office to
Shady Oaks. As was his routine, Mr. Hogan went to the club
to have lunch and practice. Peter and Willi drove out to Mr.
Hogan's practice area and spent the remaining time with him
observing his practice session. This part wasn't a question-
and-answer session. They simply watched.

Peter and Willi watched every shot in silence. Nothing
was said or asked. Willi, however, noticed that Mr. Hogan's

divots were all shallow and thin, unlike the long, deep divots produced by most players. Once Mr. Hogan had finished the session, Willi could contain himself no longer. Without notifying Kostis, Willi approached Mr. Hogan to ask his one burning question.

"Mr. Hogan, if I may, I would like to ask one question," said Willi.

Mr. Hogan nodded, and Willi continued. "Mr. Hogan, I noticed as you played your shots you hardly take a divot. Why is that?"

Hogan came back with a question of his own. "You are a golf professional, aren't you?"

"Yes," said Willi. To which Hogan responded, "Then you should know why."

Willi was taken aback by the reply and took it personally at first. No further words were exchanged. But, as Willi reflected on the answer, he realized that Mr. Hogan was not insulting him. He realized that as Mr. Hogan saw it, if you called yourself a professional, you had to clearly understand certain swing concepts. This happened to be one of them. If for some reason you didn't know the answer, you were to find it—in the dirt.

Have No Fear

Roland Harper, long-time professional at Colonial, told me he was playing in a pro-am back in his home state of Kansas with a guy from his hometown. His friend had played in pro-ams before, but he had never played with Roland in actual competition. This made the friend both excited and extremely nervous. The first few holes were brutal; the amateur friend was scattering shots everywhere. In an attempt to help his friend, Roland sidled over to him and advised, "Take a deep breath and get ahold of yourself. I've never seen you play like this."

His friend explained how badly he had wanted to play well to impress him. Roland said he listened patiently, and then put his arm around his friend's shoulder. "John," he said, "I have had the rare privilege and honor of playing a round of golf with Ben Hogan. Believe me when I tell you this. After having played with him, there is *nothing* you can do on the golf course that would impress me.

"So relax, and let's have fun."

THE SHAFT KICKER

THERE IS A BREED of golfer that experiments with club after club in an endless search for the right one. They know that every club is minutely different in size, weight, appearance and performance characteristics, even those that roll off an assembly line. Mr. Hogan was acutely aware of the inherent flaws in the manufacturing process. That's why a shaft kicker sits on the Hogan Company plant floor.

"Shaft kicker" is the name Mr. Hogan and Gene Sheeley gave to an invention that aligns the golf club's shaft with the clubhead's hosel. To understand its function and why they felt it was necessary, you must first understand a certain part of the clubmaking process.

To accommodate the shaft of the club, a hole is bored in the neck, or hosel. Although the first hole in the first clubhead is bored perfectly and the center-lines of the shaft and hosel are aligned perfectly, the hole eventually strays off-center due to the boring tool wearing out. Thus, the shaft and clubhead don't line up. The shaft kicker bends the golf shaft slightly so it lines up at the point where the shaft enters the hosel. This only applies to forged clubheads. Cast clubs are a totally different issue.

His invention holds the clubhead in two different positions. From these positions the shaft kicker realigns the shaft with the hosel if the shaft is found to be out of alignment due to a bad bore. All Hogan clubs are tested, and the imperfect ones encounter the shaft kicker.

Even though Mr. Hogan knew club manufacturing wasn't perfect, he never accepted that it had to be that way. With his shaft kicker, he gave his product and company a competitive edge. Only a person with the keenest of an eye for clubs and business would focus in these terms. That was Mr. Hogan.

WE FINALLY DISCOVER THE MISSING LINK

I RETURNED FROM NEW YORK one year with a putting training device given to me by my friend Don Edwards, a member at Winged Foot. Called "The Bickler," it consisted of a rod inserted into the small hole in the top of the grip, which was connected to a cuplike extension that fit against the right wrist. The idea was to prevent the right wrist from flexing, or "breaking down," during the stroke. Don was involved in the development and marketing of the device, and wanted me to experiment with it and show it around.

I liked The Bickler so much I decided to show it to Mr. Hogan. It was the first time I had ever shown him such a device. I walked into his office, grabbed a putter that was leaning against the wall and placed his hands around the device and onto the putter. I'm amazed still at my temerity. Imagine talking to Ben Hogan about using a training aid. And further imagine the picture of him in his suit and tie with me on one knee in front of him, rattling on about its merits.

After gabbing away a while, I finally asked, "How do you like it?"

"I *don't* like it," said Mr. Hogan. For the first time, I stepped back from my excitement and started questioning the validity of The Bickler.

Let me stress that The Bickler was extremely successful. Hundreds of name pros tried it and liked it. But because Mr. Hogan didn't like it, I knew there was a problem with it and watched Mr. Hogan closely to find out what it was. It quickly dawned on me that although The Bickler controlled the right wrist, Mr. Hogan's right-hand placement was awkward and unnatural. I could see it by the way he wrestled with his hands. As he swung his putter, his left wrist collapsed after making contact. The more he fiddled with the device, the more he disliked it.

Mr. Hogan stood up straight, took The Bickler off his

putter and handed it back to me. To be courteous, I asked him if I should get him one. "No," he said.

That evening I visited a neighbor who owned a metal fabricating shop. I gave him a sketch I'd made of modifications I'd made to The Bickler based on my observations of Mr. Hogan. We went over to his shop and built the "Missing Link," which has two arm pads as opposed to one. With the Missing Link, neither the left arm nor the right arm braces can hinge or unhinge. It has a metal stem that extends down and beside the putter grip so you can comfortably hold the device and the putter in a natural manner.

It's perfect. Thanks, Mr. Hogan.

LIGHTS, CAMERA . . . AND SAY A PRAYER

HANK ROJAS TOLD ME that in 1987 the Hogan Company needed a new TV commercial. The company had not featured Mr. Hogan as the principal character in an advertising spot in years, but it was decided that his personal presence would do much to give the company a boost.

They decided to shoot the commercial at Rivera Country Club in Los Angeles. Once everyone arrived, they found a spot, set everything up, and asked Mr. Hogan to get warmed up. Looking elegant in a long-sleeve yellow sweater, gray slacks and his traditional white cap, he complied.

At the time, Mr. Hogan was 74 years old and long past his daily practice sessions at Shady Oaks. Going into the video shoot, there had been much apprehension from the production people as to the toll the years might have taken on his swing. The last thing anyone wanted was a frail-looking Hogan.

Mr. Hogan dropped three balls on the ground. He then proceeded to blade the first shot, hit the second poorly and bladed the third. Although the camera was not following the ball, the swing clearly didn't look right.

Mr. Hogan looked over at Hank and said, "I'm ready."

Mr. Hogan was given his cue. With the cameras rolling, he addressed the ball, made a beautiful swing and produced a perfectly struck shot. Hank was stunned. They turned off the cameras and went back to Fort Worth with a classic piece of film.

Having built a swing that could hold up under pressure, Mr. Hogan rose to the occasion once again.

15

The Silent Benefactor

EVERY PROFESSIONAL ATHLETE, celebrity and public figure is indebted to Francis Sullivan and Ben Hogan. Their efforts in a little-known court case helped ensure that endorsement income paid to these professionals comes unchallenged.

In 1957, Sullivan, a Philadelphia trial lawyer, won a court case concerning a company's obligation to pay a person for the use of his likeness for commercial gain. It is a landmark decision, for athletes and celebrities today receive huge sums of money in exchange for the use of their names and likenesses. At the center of the case was none other than Ben Hogan.

This ruling was significant, and it has only gained in importance as the years have moved on and the stakes grown larger. Prior to *Hogan* v. *A. S. Barnes & Company, Incorporated*, most companies who wanted to use a celebrity to endorse one of their products did offer compensation. However, it was also possible for a company to use a celebrity's likeness to make it look as if he were endorsing a product without paying him.

You may be wondering why you haven't heard about the

case before. It's because the court cases that are printed in those massive books attorneys use for research are cases that have been appealed or have significant case law issues tied to them. The cases that are tried, but never appealed, don't get published. Thus they are relegated to obscurity.

I did not hear about this noteworthy event from Mr. Hogan. I heard about it from Sullivan himself at the Merion Golf Club in Ardmore, Pennsylvania. I met Sullivan in Merion's upstairs TV room on a beautiful Saturday afternoon. I had just finished my round and was resting for a few minutes before heading out to work on my game.

As I was resting on a couch, a gentleman came down the stairs and into the TV room. I looked up, and we exchanged greetings. He eyed one of the padded lounge chairs and asked, "Do you mind if I watch the TV with you?"

"Of course not," I said and got up to formally and politely introduce myself.

As he sat down in his chair, he remarked that he noticed my accent and asked me where I was from. I responded by saying, "Fort Worth, Texas."

"Oh, really!" he replied. "Where do you play your golf?"

"Colonial Country Club," I said.

"Do you happen to know Ben Hogan?" he asked.

"Why yes, I know Mr. Hogan very well. In fact, I grew up shagging golf balls for him at Shady Oaks Country Club. Why, do you know him?"

"Yes, I do," he said.

In fact, Sullivan knew him well. For the next hour I

learned what the name Ben Hogan meant to sports in general. I've heard people remark that Mr. Hogan seldom gave back to the game of golf. Well, after you hear this story, you'll never have that thought again.

Francis Sullivan was a frail, smallish man with thin, graying hair. He appeared to be in his late 70s and didn't strike me as the picture of a prominent Philadelphia trial lawyer that he was. He was almost Southern in his manner, very formal and polite. I felt as if I should sit up straight, and talk and listen with care.

Sullivan began by explaining that he was once Mr. Hogan's attorney and still attended to a few of his business needs. He said that when the legal minds back in the 1950s were considering the merits of making a case for celebrities to be paid for the use of their name and likeness, they spent many hours discussing whom they should build the case around.

Athletes from every sport were mentioned. From Joe DiMaggio to Red Grange, every big name in every major sport—football, baseball, basketball, track and field, golf— was considered. They chose to approach Ben Hogan.

In their opinion, of all the athletes of his day, Mr. Hogan was the one with the prestige, integrity and populist appeal to afford Sullivan the greatest chance for a courtroom victory.

In the case, Mr. Hogan sued a book publisher for using his name and likeness in a book, *Golfing with the Masters,* in such a way that gave the false impression that Mr. Hogan had participated in the preparation of the book. Hogan sued and won on the grounds of unfair competition.

Part of the ruling reads: "There can be no doubt that Ben Hogan has acquired over many years a unique position and reputation in the sport of golf. This position has been acquired by virtue of a tremendous amount of work, ability and perseverance on his part. As a result, his name and photograph in connection with any aspect of the sport of golf have great commercial value. Defendant, well realizing this fact, has unfairly attempted to profit from it."

In deciding the damages to be paid to Mr. Hogan, the judge took into account the evidence of how important outside earnings were to Mr. Hogan. While Hogan had made approximately one million dollars through golf since 1937, it was significant that only one quarter of those earnings ($250,000) came from tournament prize money. The remaining three quarters of Hogan's income ($750,000) were from endorsements, royalties, exhibitions, magazine articles, personal appearances and motion pictures.

It's mildly ironic that the company Hogan was suing, A. S. Barnes & Company, was actually his own publisher. In 1948, Barnes published Hogan's *Power Golf,* from which Hogan earned $62,950 in royalties up to 1957. And, in the same year this case was decided, Barnes published the first edition of Hogan's better known *Five Lessons.*

On June 19, 1957, the judge decided in Mr. Hogan's favor and awarded him compensatory damages in the sum of $5,000.

The decision read in part: "From this evidence there emerges the clear conclusions (a) that, by reason of plaintiff's unique position in the world of golf, publications on the subject of his golfing style and technique are a source of substantial income to him; and (b) that a publisher who makes an unauthorized use of such assets and appropriates them to his own commercial purposes, subjects himself to the payment of damages."

Why did Mr. Hogan agree to be the one to try to set the precedent? To him, the book was an intrusion into his privacy that was unwanted and without merit. He was, of course, distrustful of writers in general. He also was very particular about his name being associated with any statements having to do with how to play the game of golf. For example, Herbert Warren Wind has commented numerous times about how detailed and painstakingly thorough Hogan was in editing the *Five Lessons* book.

The implications and consequences of the case were serious indeed. But there's a comical side as well. Before the case went to trial, the author of the book tried to get Hogan's permission to validate the material before the book went to press. The author sent Mr. Hogan a packet containing settlement information, a release letter for him to sign away all his rights and the promise of $100 once the release letter was returned, plus two *free* copies of the book when completed.

Mr. Hogan's reply was a letter containing three words: "Are you kidding?"

A few weeks after returning from Merion and my conversation with Sullivan, I drove over to Mr. Hogan's office. I brought up my conversation with Sullivan and the court case. I said I was shocked that nobody knew about the case. To my surprise, the case seemed all but forgotten to him. As usual, he didn't elaborate.

When I said that Sullivan made me promise to say hello, Mr. Hogan looked off to the side for a brief few seconds, as though reflecting on something distant and long forgotten. He smiled and turned back to face me and said, "I should call Francis."

16

Looking Back

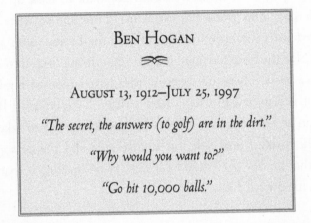

BEN HOGAN

AUGUST 13, 1912–JULY 25, 1997

"The secret, the answers (to golf) are in the dirt."

"Why would you want to?"

"Go hit 10,000 balls."

THE FURTHER I WALK through life the more I appreciate what Mr. Hogan told me. His words mean more to me each and every day. It's about much more than just how to hit a golf ball. What he said reaches deep into my very heart and soul. It was his way of saying to me it must come from within. The search for excellence in whatever you chose to do begins and ends with you.

Life has been more than kind to me. Everywhere I turn, I see opportunities I never dreamed of as I was growing up. I was more than happy to make 95 cents an hour doing a job I loved. Add to that the reality that I was going to spend hours a day in the presence of the greatest golfer to have ever lived. Then ask yourself, what more could be in store? As a friend once told me, if you want to compare stats, let's go. My money is on Hogan. It's a tough case to argue against.

We live in an amazing world, a great country and during a wonderful time in history. Couple this with the experiences of family and friends and I would not want to back up one single day. This book has taken me a lifetime to write. It started with the opportunities offered me by my mom and dad. Not the financial ones, but the ones driven deep into my will to grow. There are so many who have added to my life and it is reflected in what I have written. I experienced Ben Hogan at his emotional height. The world was his to take. I saw his professional side, his human side and the personal side that no one else could have seen. How amazing is that?

I liked what I saw.

ACKNOWLEDGMENTS

THIS IS A BOOK of Ben Hogan stories. Some are mine. Others belong to those I have known and called friends. They're worth reading or telling depending on how many margaritas we have time for.

Those responsible for this are many. Consider this. At 17 years old, I happened to be in a geometry class sitting with a kid who was leaving town and trying to find somebody to fill his job slot! I happened to be in a position where I needed a job for the summer. I happened to care that it involved golf.

Now, fast forward.

I happened to be fortunate enough to join a club, Colonial Country Club, continue a lifelong relationship with my Ben Hogan Company friends, travel the world making more friends, have a reason to continue to visit with Mr. Hogan and most important, recognize the value of all this.

The stories, as you see, started many years ago. Often, I thought of how to tell them. It wasn't until that trip to the airport when Nick Faldo said to me, "You should write a book," and John Simpson said, "You should keep it in the context of your youth." It was then and only then that I realized this was a task worth the effort.

Nothing like this is simple. Guy Yocom told me that. Early on in this project, I tried to convince Guy to write the book with me. For many reasons he didn't have the time, but in the end, he made the time. He wrapped his arms around the manuscript, pulling everything together. His passion for Hogan, golf and history shows in how he developed the final text. He's glad he gave it a second look.

Many years ago, Mr. Hogan said that his ideal book would be written by a woman telling the first part of his story and a man finishing up with the technical side. Never in my wildest dreams did I think that I would end up using that approach. It was not by design. If I hadn't been introduced to Jill Colford, I don't know how this book would have gotten to print. She took my scattered tales and pulled them together in a meaningful fashion. We spent many an hour going back and forth striving to create a book that would live forever. It will. And her dedication to it clearly shows. We are both sorry the task has come to an end. But, without a doubt, had she done anything less than pour her fullest effort into the project none of this would have moved forward.

It wouldn't be fair to not mention Paul Lipp. Guy explained to me that the accompanying art had to be just right. But, who to do it? Guy held his breath and said . . . Paul Lipp. His pencil sketches are classic. I only wish I could have had him do more. He is truly blessed with a talent from God.

There are three key individuals: Scott Waxman, Bill Shinker

and Erin Moore, that must be mentioned for the simple reason that although this book is a form of art it is very much still a business venture. Someone has to recognize the value of all this so the stories can be shared. I am not a writer in the traditional sense. I told a story, probably the only one I'll ever tell in this form. The world of publishing was a fog to me (and still is).

Scott, bless his soul, quickly understood the strength of what is written here. Without seeing the whole text, he reached back into his significant knowledge of the book business and knew exactly who would want the publishing rights. His experience as an agent was invaluable in moving through the maze of endless conversations. Everyone had told me how difficult this would be. He made it easier than I could have ever imagined.

The only house Scott took the manuscript to was Gotham, or, more accurately, Bill Shinker. Bill didn't hesitate at all. It takes a good business mind to understand its markets. Bill's success in recognizing this made all our lives simpler. But to move from a handshake to a final product takes focus and direction. That could only be Erin. She guided us from the very first edit to the final word. Her calm nature and patience gave one and all the ability to relax knowing Erin's got it.

As for my friends at Hogan, we love the legacy he left. Ronnie McGraw and I go back a ways and that's fun to reflect on. Steve Dreyer, Leon Taylor, Roger West, Sharon Rae and I often talk about the "old man" and how it was on Pafford Street before it was only about the money. Nick Raffaele and I think in terms of what Mr. Hogan believed was right about golf clubs, playing golf and the business of golf. It's great to have friends!

Personally, I would not have written this if it were not for my three sons: Lee, Matt and Lance. They are my life. For many years they have listened to my stories, asking me to tell them to their friends. I think by writing these down in this way they will have them for generations to come. As with Mr. Hogan, I will strive for excellence in those things I choose to do and hopefully leave this place a better place than when I came.

And last, their mother. Vicki Nell Abrams Vasquez and I have shared a lifetime together. She has shared some of these moments and listened to the rest. Life is an easier road to travel when you can do it with someone you love.

Thank God, she doesn't mind that I play lots of golf.